Trumponomics
How America's New Leader Can Shape Global Markets and Prosperity

Table of Contents

Introduction 5

Chapter 1 The Foundations of Trumponomics 7

    Understanding Trump's Economic Philosophy 8

    The Shift from Globalism to Nationalism 11

    Key Policies Shaping the Economy 14

Chapter 2 Economic Nationalism and Global Trade 18

    Trade Wars and Tariffs: Impact on Global Trade 19

    Re-defining Trade Deals: The USMCA Example 22

    America's Position in the World Trade Order 26

Chapter 3 Tax Reform and Economic Growth 30

    The Tax Cuts and Jobs Act 31

    Effects on Businesses and Individuals 35

    Can Tax Cuts Fuel Sustainable Growth? 38

Chapter 4 The Role of Deregulation in Economic 42

    Unleashing the Private Sector 43

    Impact on Industries: Energy, Banking, and Technology 47

    Balancing Regulation and Market Freedom 51

Chapter 5 The Future of American Jobs in a 55

Revitalizing Manufacturing: Jobs vs. Automation 57

The Gig Economy and Freelance Workforce 60

Education and Skills Development for the Future 63

Chapter 6 Infrastructure Investment and Economic 67

The Plan for Rebuilding America's Infrastructure 68

Public-Private Partnerships: A New Economic Model 72

Economic Impact of Modernizing Infrastructure 75

Chapter 7 The Role of Immigration in Economic Growth. 80

Immigrant Labor and Its Contribution to Prosperity 81

Trumponomics vs. Immigration Reform 85

The Economic Debate: Protectionism or Inclusivity? 89

Chapter 8 The Impact on Global Markets and 94

US-China Trade Relations and the Global Economy 95

America's Influence on Emerging Markets 99

Trumponomics and Global Stability 103

Chapter 9 Managing Debt and Fiscal Responsibility 107

The National Debt: Is Trumponomics Sustainable? 108

Budget Cuts vs. Investment in Growth 112

The Future of America's Fiscal Policies 115

Chapter 10 Looking Ahead: A New Era of Global 118

The Legacy of Trumponomics 119

Potential Risks and Rewards for Global Markets 122

Conclusion **126**

Introduction

The rise of Trumponomics marks a significant shift in America's approach to both domestic and global economic policy. Under the leadership of Donald Trump, the U.S. moved towards an economic philosophy that prioritized national interests, economic growth, and job creation over traditional globalist strategies. This new economic agenda was characterized by aggressive tax cuts, deregulation, and an inward focus on reviving American industries. Trump's vision was clear: put America first, protect American workers, and create a business-friendly environment that would boost prosperity across the nation. While controversial to some, Trumponomics introduced a bold approach to how a country's economic health can be shaped by its leadership.

At the heart of Trumponomics lies a fundamental departure from the internationalist policies that had long governed the global order. This shift is most evident in the trade policies, which emphasized renegotiating trade deals and imposing tariffs on foreign goods. By challenging long-standing agreements like NAFTA and seeking fairer trade terms with countries like China, Trump sought to rebalance the scales in favor of American workers and businesses. While these actions sparked tensions with global trade partners, they underscored a broader vision of asserting America's dominance in the global marketplace, even if it meant disrupting the status quo.

However, the influence of Trumponomics extends beyond trade and regulation—it touches on how America views its own prosperity in a rapidly changing world. While critics argue that the focus on protectionism and the rollback of international agreements could hurt the global economy, Trump's supporters argue that his policies created an environment that nurtured American entrepreneurship and revitalized key industries. As we explore the principles of Trumponomics, it's clear that this new era is not just about America's place in the world; it's about redefining the very notion of prosperity and the role a nation's leadership plays in shaping its future.

Chapter 1
The Foundations of Trumponomics

Trumponomics is grounded in the belief that economic policies should directly benefit American citizens, with a primary focus on boosting domestic industries and securing long-term prosperity for the country. At its core, Trumponomics challenges conventional economic theories that have dominated both American politics and global markets for decades. By prioritizing the interests of American workers and businesses, this approach has brought about sweeping changes in taxation, trade, and regulation. Understanding these foundational elements is key to grasping the broad implications of Trumponomics, not just for the U.S., but for the world.

A central pillar of Trumponomics is economic nationalism, which stresses the need for the U.S. to protect its industries from foreign competition. This mindset led to a series of policies aimed at reshaping America's role in global trade, including a redefinition of trade agreements and the introduction of tariffs on imports. By pushing for fairer trade terms, President Trump sought to reverse what he perceived as decades of economic disadvantage for the United States. These policies were grounded in the idea that America's prosperity should no longer be tied to the global market's whims, but instead driven by policies that directly protect and benefit the nation's economy.

The framework of Trumponomics also emphasizes reducing government intervention in business, enabling the private sector to thrive through deregulation and tax cuts. By significantly lowering corporate tax rates and rolling back federal regulations, the administration aimed to provide businesses with the freedom to grow, innovate, and create jobs. This combination of policies marked a dramatic shift away from the Obama-era approach, which was characterized by an emphasis on government oversight and global cooperation. The goal was clear: create an environment where American companies can compete on a global scale while fostering economic growth that benefits the entire country.

Understanding Trump's Economic Philosophy

Donald Trump's economic philosophy, often referred to as Trumponomics, is characterized by a combination of nationalism, deregulation, tax cuts, and protectionist policies, all designed to prioritize the interests of the American economy. His approach is driven by the fundamental belief that the U.S. should take a more assertive stance in global trade and reduce its reliance on international agreements that, in his view, disadvantage American workers and businesses. At its core, Trump's economic philosophy is built around the concept of "America First," which calls for economic policies that put the prosperity of the American people above all else.

One of the central tenets of Trumponomics is economic nationalism, which advocates for policies that protect domestic industries from foreign competition. This idea is rooted in the belief that globalization, as it has been practiced in the past, often harms American workers by outsourcing jobs and creating trade imbalances. To address these issues, Trump introduced policies such as imposing tariffs on imports, renegotiating trade agreements, and pulling out of international deals that he argued were not beneficial to the U.S. This was most evident in his approach to the North American Free Trade Agreement (NAFTA), which he replaced with the United States-Mexico-Canada Agreement (USMCA), and his trade war with China, which led to the imposition of tariffs on billions of dollars' worth of Chinese goods. By doing so, he aimed to level the playing field, encouraging businesses to move production back to the U.S. and creating jobs in industries that had previously been outsourced.

Another key element of Trump's economic philosophy is deregulation. He consistently argued that excessive government regulation stifles innovation and economic growth. Throughout his presidency, Trump sought to reduce the regulatory burden on American businesses, particularly in industries such as energy, banking, and manufacturing. The idea behind this was that by cutting red tape, businesses would have greater freedom to operate, innovate, and hire more workers. Trump's administration rolled back numerous Obama-era regulations, including environmental protections, labor laws, and financial regulations that were seen as barriers to economic growth. By championing deregulation, Trump hoped to create a more business-friendly environment that would foster entrepreneurship, increase competition, and ultimately lead to higher wages and more job opportunities for Americans.

Tax cuts were another cornerstone of Trump's economic philosophy. The Tax Cuts and Jobs Act, signed into law in December 2017, was one of his major legislative accomplishments. This tax reform aimed to reduce the corporate tax rate from 35% to 21% and provided temporary tax cuts for individuals. The rationale behind this move was to stimulate economic growth by putting more money into the hands of businesses and consumers. Proponents of the tax cuts argued that reducing the corporate tax rate would encourage companies to invest in the U.S., expand operations, and create jobs. However, critics contended that the benefits of these tax cuts primarily went to the wealthiest Americans and large corporations, leading to an increase in the national debt. Nevertheless, the cuts were viewed by many as a crucial part of Trump's strategy to boost economic growth and make the U.S. more competitive globally.

A final pillar of Trump's economic philosophy is his focus on energy independence. Under his administration, the U.S. became the world's top producer of oil and natural gas, thanks in large part to the expansion of domestic drilling and the loosening of restrictions on fossil fuel production. Trump's emphasis on energy independence was motivated by both economic and national security concerns. By reducing America's reliance on foreign energy sources, he believed that the U.S. could not only lower its trade deficit but also enhance its geopolitical power. The expansion of the oil and gas industry also created jobs, especially in rural areas, where drilling operations were often located. This focus on energy production, along with the president's skepticism of climate change policies, led to tensions with environmental groups and many Democratic lawmakers.

In summary, Trump's economic philosophy is built on a combination of protectionism, deregulation, tax cuts, and energy independence. His policies were designed to shift the balance of power in favor of American workers, businesses, and industries. While critics argue that Trumponomics disproportionately benefited the wealthy and ignored environmental and social considerations, supporters contend that it revitalized American manufacturing, stimulated economic growth, and reshaped the global economic order to better suit the U.S.'s national interests.

The Shift from Globalism to Nationalism

The shift from globalism to nationalism under Donald Trump's leadership represents one of the most dramatic changes in U.S. economic and foreign policy in recent decades. This shift has had profound implications not only for America's domestic policy but also for its relationship with the rest of the world. For much of the post-World War II era, the United States championed globalism—advocating for free trade, international cooperation, and global institutions. Globalism saw the U.S. as a leader in a world that was interconnected through trade, politics, and shared norms. However, under Trump's administration, the United States adopted a nationalist approach, emphasizing sovereignty, self-reliance, and policies that favored the nation's economic and strategic interests over global cooperation.

At the heart of this transition was Trump's belief that America had been taken advantage of in many international deals, leading to a perception of economic and political disadvantage. Under globalism, trade agreements such as the North American Free Trade Agreement (NAFTA), the World Trade Organization (WTO), and various United Nations (UN) agreements were designed to promote international cooperation and economic integration. While these agreements were created to open markets and increase global trade, Trump argued that they disproportionately benefited other countries, particularly China and Mexico, at the expense of American workers and businesses. By focusing on national interests and pushing for "America First" policies, Trump sought to redress what he viewed as unfair trade practices and to restore the competitive edge of the U.S. economy.

One of the most visible aspects of this shift was Trump's approach to trade. He believed that the U.S. should move away from multilateral agreements in favor of bilateral deals that put American interests first. This led to the renegotiation of NAFTA, which Trump replaced with the United States-Mexico-Canada Agreement (USMCA). The new agreement included provisions aimed at increasing American manufacturing, improving labor standards, and addressing trade imbalances with Mexico and Canada. Trump also withdrew the U.S. from the Trans-Pacific Partnership (TPP), a trade deal that was intended to strengthen economic ties with Asia. Trump's move was a clear rejection of the globalist vision of interdependence, opting instead for a more protectionist and self-interested approach to trade.

Perhaps the most contentious element of Trump's nationalist policies was the trade war with China. Trump imposed tariffs on Chinese imports in an effort to reduce the U.S. trade deficit with China and to press for changes in Chinese trade practices, including intellectual property theft and forced technology transfers. The tariffs were part of a broader effort to decouple the U.S. from China's growing economic influence, shifting from a strategy of engagement and integration to one of competition and confrontation. While critics argued that tariffs would hurt American consumers and businesses by increasing the cost of imports, Trump maintained that the long-term benefits would outweigh the short-term disruptions, as they would bring jobs back to America and protect domestic industries.

The nationalism that Trump promoted also extended to the realm of immigration. Under globalism, immigration was seen as a source of diversity, talent, and economic growth. However, Trump framed immigration through the lens of national security and economic protectionism. He pushed for stricter border controls, sought to build a wall along the U.S.-Mexico border, and implemented policies that reduced the number of immigrants allowed into the country. The rationale behind these policies was the belief that unchecked immigration, particularly illegal immigration, had negative effects on wages, jobs, and public services for American citizens. Trump argued that focusing on national security and restricting immigration would help preserve American jobs, reduce crime, and maintain the cultural integrity of the nation.

Nationalism also reshaped U.S. foreign policy, with Trump's "America First" stance challenging the global leadership role the U.S. had played since World War II. Trump's skepticism toward international institutions like the United Nations, NATO, and the World Health Organization (WHO) was a key aspect of his nationalist approach. He argued that these organizations often worked to the disadvantage of the U.S. and that the U.S. should reduce its financial commitments and involvement in global affairs unless it directly benefited American interests. The U.S. withdrawal from the Paris Climate Agreement, the Iran nuclear deal, and the UNESCO treaty further underscored his administration's retreat from multilateralism in favor of a more isolated and self-focused approach.

In conclusion, the shift from globalism to nationalism under Trump marked a turning point in U.S. policy, characterized by an emphasis on protecting American interests, reducing global entanglements, and prioritizing domestic industries and jobs. This shift has been met with both support and criticism, as it fundamentally altered the country's role on the world stage. While proponents argue that nationalism has strengthened America's economic position and sovereignty, critics contend that it has undermined international cooperation and global stability. Regardless, Trump's embrace of nationalism has reshaped the economic and political landscape, and its impact will likely be felt for years to come.

Key Policies Shaping the Economy

Donald Trump's presidency brought about a series of key policies that fundamentally reshaped the U.S. economy, with a focus on deregulation, tax reform, protectionism, and a shift towards energy independence. These policies were driven by the central idea of *America First*, with the aim of boosting economic growth, creating jobs, and protecting domestic industries. While these policies were often controversial and sparked intense debates, they marked a distinct departure from previous administrations and set the tone for the U.S. economic approach during Trump's tenure.

Tax Reform and Economic Growth

One of the cornerstone achievements of Trump's economic policy was the Tax Cuts and Jobs Act of 2017, which dramatically altered the U.S. tax system. The bill aimed to reduce taxes for individuals and corporations, with the goal of stimulating economic growth by increasing investment, job creation, and consumer spending. Corporate tax rates were slashed from 35% to 21%, one of the largest reductions in U.S. history. The idea behind this was to make American businesses more competitive globally and encourage them to bring jobs and investments back to the U.S. The corporate tax cut was also seen as a way to reward companies for repatriating overseas profits, which would potentially create more jobs and raise wages.

In addition to the corporate tax cuts, the Tax Cuts and Jobs Act also included tax cuts for individuals, although these cuts were temporary and set to expire in 2025. The law doubled the standard deduction and reduced tax brackets for most Americans, aiming to leave more disposable income in the hands of consumers. Proponents of the tax reform argued that it would lead to higher economic growth, while critics claimed that the benefits were skewed toward the wealthiest Americans and large corporations, potentially exacerbating income inequality and increasing the national deficit.

Deregulation and Business Freedom

Another key policy shaping the economy during Trump's presidency was the emphasis on deregulation. Trump believed that excessive government regulation was a major barrier to economic growth, particularly in industries such as energy, finance, and healthcare. As part of his deregulatory agenda, Trump signed executive orders aimed at cutting down on the number of federal regulations, with a goal of eliminating two regulations for every new one introduced. The administration argued that reducing red tape would allow businesses to grow more freely, create jobs, and invest in innovation.

One of the most significant deregulatory actions was in the energy sector. The Trump administration rolled back numerous environmental regulations, including the Clean Power Plan, which aimed to reduce greenhouse gas emissions from power plants. By loosening these restrictions, Trump aimed to increase domestic energy production, particularly through fossil fuels such as coal, oil, and natural gas. This was in line with Trump's focus on energy independence, as the U.S. became the world's top producer of oil and natural gas during his presidency. While supporters argued that deregulation in the energy sector led to job creation and lower energy costs, critics raised concerns about environmental degradation and the long-term impacts of fossil fuel reliance.

Protectionism and Trade Policies

Trump's protectionist trade policies were another significant element of his economic agenda. Under the banner of "America First," Trump sought to reduce the U.S. trade deficit and bring jobs back to America by renegotiating existing trade deals and imposing tariffs on foreign goods. The most notable example of this was the trade war with China, where Trump implemented tariffs on billions of dollars' worth of Chinese imports, accusing China of unfair trade practices, intellectual property theft, and currency manipulation. The tariffs were aimed at encouraging China to open its markets further and stop practices that Trump argued were damaging to American workers.

In addition to the China tariffs, Trump sought to renegotiate trade agreements that he believed were disadvantageous to the U.S., including the North American Free Trade Agreement (NAFTA). The U.S.-Mexico-Canada Agreement (USMCA), which replaced NAFTA, included provisions to increase American manufacturing, strengthen labor rights, and improve access to markets for U.S. farmers and manufacturers. Trump's approach to trade was centered on the idea of fairness, arguing that past trade deals had allowed other countries to exploit the U.S. While critics argued that protectionist policies would harm global trade and increase prices for American consumers, Trump maintained that these measures were necessary to restore American economic power and job security.

Energy Independence and Infrastructure Investment

A central component of Trump's economic policy was the drive for energy independence. His administration worked to increase domestic energy production by expanding oil and gas drilling, particularly in shale regions, and loosening environmental regulations that had previously restricted fossil fuel extraction. This focus on energy independence was seen as a way to reduce the U.S.'s reliance on foreign oil and enhance national security. The U.S. became the world's leading producer of oil during Trump's presidency, an achievement that many saw as a victory for his economic agenda.

Trump also advocated for large-scale infrastructure investment as a means of stimulating economic growth. While the ambitious infrastructure plan that Trump proposed never fully materialized, his administration worked on various projects aimed at improving transportation, broadband, and energy infrastructure. Trump argued that investing in modernizing the nation's infrastructure would create jobs, boost productivity, and improve the country's competitiveness globally.

Trump's key policies—tax reform, deregulation, protectionist trade measures, and energy independence—were designed with the goal of reshaping the U.S. economy to focus on domestic growth, job creation, and national self-sufficiency. These policies marked a clear departure from the globalist, free-market approach that had dominated U.S. economic policy for decades. While these policies generated significant debate and criticism, they undeniably reshaped the landscape of American economic strategy, leaving a lasting impact on industries, workers, and the nation's position in the global economy.

Chapter 2
Economic Nationalism and Global Trade

Economic nationalism, a key principle of Trumponomics, represents a sharp shift from the globalist policies that have traditionally governed U.S. trade relations. At the core of economic nationalism is the belief that national interests—particularly those of domestic workers, industries, and businesses—should take precedence over international agreements and cooperation. This philosophy challenges the decades-long consensus that globalization and free trade are beneficial for all countries involved. For President Trump, economic nationalism meant renegotiating trade deals to ensure that they benefitted American workers and businesses, and, where necessary, imposing tariffs on foreign goods to protect domestic industries. The goal was clear: to restore America's economic power and secure a better deal for U.S. citizens, especially those in manufacturing sectors who felt left behind by the forces of global trade.

One of the most significant manifestations of Trump's economic nationalism was his approach to global trade agreements. Trump believed that previous trade deals, such as the North American Free Trade Agreement (NAFTA), had resulted in massive trade deficits and the outsourcing of American jobs to countries with lower labor costs. As part of his "America First" strategy, he sought to either renegotiate or withdraw from these agreements. The renegotiation of

NAFTA, which culminated in the United States-Mexico-Canada Agreement (USMCA), was a key moment in his trade policy. The USMCA included provisions designed to boost U.S. manufacturing, enforce stronger labor standards, and open new markets for American farmers. Trump's insistence on revising existing trade agreements was part of a broader effort to recalibrate global trade in favor of American interests and to ensure that future trade arrangements were more balanced.

The second major aspect of Trump's economic nationalism was his trade war with China, which epitomized the president's protectionist stance. Trump's administration imposed tariffs on billions of dollars' worth of Chinese goods, aiming to reduce the U.S. trade deficit with China, protect American intellectual property, and press China to reform its trade practices. The tariffs, which sparked retaliatory measures from China, led to significant disruptions in global supply chains. While critics argued that these measures would harm American consumers by raising prices and could damage the global economy, Trump and his supporters believed that they were necessary steps to restore fair trade practices and bring manufacturing jobs back to the U.S. This chapter will explore the key moments of Trump's economic nationalism, analyzing the impact of his trade policies on both the U.S. economy and global trade dynamics, and examining whether his strategy of protectionism and renegotiation was successful in achieving its stated goals.

Trade Wars and Tariffs: Impact on Global Trade

The trade wars and tariffs initiated under Donald Trump's administration represented a fundamental shift in the United States' approach to international trade. Driven by an economic nationalist philosophy, Trump aimed to reduce the U.S. trade deficit, bring back manufacturing jobs, and protect American industries from unfair foreign competition. The most prominent example of this approach was the trade war with China, which had far-reaching implications not just for the two countries involved, but for global trade as a whole.

Trump's primary tool in the trade war was the imposition of tariffs—taxes placed on imported goods. In 2018, he announced tariffs on steel and aluminum imports from various countries, including China, citing national security concerns and the desire to protect American industries from what he argued were predatory trade practices. The tariffs on Chinese goods were especially significant, with tariffs imposed on billions of dollars' worth of Chinese products, including electronics, machinery, and consumer goods. The aim was to reduce the U.S. trade deficit with China, which Trump viewed as one of the major economic imbalances caused by unfair trade practices. The U.S. government argued that China's practices, such as forced technology transfers and intellectual property theft, were contributing to the trade imbalance and damaging American industries.

The tariffs imposed on Chinese goods were met with retaliatory tariffs from China, creating a back-and-forth escalation that lasted for several years. Chinese tariffs targeted U.S. agricultural products, particularly soybeans, pork, and other goods, which caused immediate financial distress for American farmers who were highly dependent on exports to China. The trade war led to disruptions in global supply chains as companies that had become reliant on cheap Chinese manufacturing found themselves facing higher costs and having to find new sources of supply. This shift in trade dynamics created uncertainty for businesses worldwide, as global trade flows were altered and industries adjusted to new cost structures.

While the trade war initially sparked fears of a broader global recession, its longer-term effects were more nuanced. In some cases, it prompted U.S. companies to reconsider their dependence on Chinese manufacturing. As tariffs made Chinese goods more expensive, some companies moved production to other countries with lower labor costs, such as Vietnam, Mexico, and India. While this allowed some businesses to reduce their tariff burdens, it also introduced new challenges, as firms had to navigate the complexities of new supply chains, differing regulatory environments, and, in some cases, a lack of the same level of infrastructure and expertise found in China.

Global markets also experienced volatility due to the trade war, as international businesses scrambled to adjust to the shifting landscape. As tariffs were introduced, the prices of goods on both sides increased, leading to higher production costs for companies and, in many cases, higher prices for consumers. In some industries, like the automotive sector, tariffs led to price increases for consumers in both the U.S. and abroad, which hurt demand. At the same time, countries outside the U.S. and China were caught in the crossfire, particularly those in the Asia-Pacific region that were dependent on trade with both economic superpowers. Nations like Japan, South Korea, and the European Union found themselves navigating the complexities of a rapidly changing global trading system, trying to shield their economies from the fallout of the trade war.

The U.S. tariffs on Chinese imports also pushed China to take retaliatory measures, not only by imposing tariffs on U.S. goods but by seeking to strengthen its trade relationships with other countries. China pursued trade deals with the European Union, Latin American nations, and African countries, creating a more diversified trade network that allowed it to reduce its dependency on the U.S. market.

As a result, China's global economic influence continued to grow despite the tariff war.

The trade war also had broader implications for international institutions and agreements. Trump's "America First" approach led to skepticism about the effectiveness of multilateral trade agreements like the World Trade Organization (WTO), as the administration argued that these institutions were not equipped to handle the unfair trade practices of rising powers like China. This skepticism was reflected in the U.S. decision to block the appointment of judges to the WTO's Appellate Body, which rendered the institution less effective in resolving trade disputes.

In conclusion, the trade wars and tariffs implemented by Trump had a profound impact on global trade. While the trade war with China was the most visible example, the ripple effects of the tariffs were felt across the world, creating uncertainty in global markets and disrupting established supply chains. The tariffs also forced many companies to reconsider their manufacturing strategies and explore alternative trade relationships, leading to the restructuring of global trade flows. Although Trump's trade policies were meant to protect American workers and industries, the longer-term effects on the global economy were complex, revealing both opportunities and challenges in the shifting dynamics of international trade.

Re-defining Trade Deals: The USMCA Example

The United States-Mexico-Canada Agreement (USMCA) represents one of the most significant redefinitions of trade deals under the Trump administration, reflecting the shift from traditional globalist policies to a more nationalist, protectionist approach. The USMCA replaced the North American Free Trade Agreement (NAFTA), which had been in place since 1994 and was widely seen as a cornerstone of global trade in North America. The USMCA, however, was not merely a rebranding of NAFTA—it was an attempt to reshape the terms of trade between the three countries to better align with the economic priorities of the Trump administration, particularly with regard to U.S. manufacturing, labor standards, and trade imbalances.

Trump's primary goal in renegotiating NAFTA was to reduce the U.S. trade deficit with both Mexico and Canada, a key issue that he repeatedly emphasized throughout his campaign. NAFTA, in Trump's view, had led to the outsourcing of American jobs, particularly in manufacturing sectors like automotive and textiles, which had caused job losses and wage stagnation for U.S. workers. In his pursuit of "America First" economic policies, Trump aimed to renegotiate trade terms that would restore U.S. competitiveness and ensure that American workers benefited more from North American trade. This meant implementing changes that would directly impact the flow of goods, labor standards, and even intellectual property protections across the three countries.

The USMCA introduced a number of provisions that directly benefited U.S. industries and workers. One of the most significant changes was in the automotive sector. Under the USMCA, a higher percentage of automobile parts must be sourced from within the U.S., Canada, or Mexico—up from 62.5% under NAFTA to 75%. This change aimed to encourage the production of more car parts in North America, thereby creating jobs and reducing the reliance on overseas manufacturers. The agreement also introduced a provision that requires a portion of car manufacturing to be done by workers earning at least $16 per hour. This provision was a direct response to concerns about wage disparities between the U.S. and Mexican workers, which had been seen as a contributing factor to the outsourcing of jobs to Mexico under NAFTA. The hope was that by raising wages for Mexican workers in the automotive sector, the trade balance would become more equitable for U.S. manufacturers.

Labor standards were another focus of the USMCA renegotiations. The new agreement included stronger labor provisions aimed at improving workers' rights in all three countries, particularly in Mexico, where labor conditions had been a contentious issue under NAFTA. The USMCA included mechanisms to enforce labor standards and address concerns about workers' rights, including a provision that allowed for the establishment of an independent panel to oversee labor disputes. These changes were designed to prevent a race to the bottom in terms of labor standards, which was a frequent criticism of NAFTA, and to ensure that workers in all three countries had fair wages and working conditions.

Another important aspect of the USMCA was its updates to intellectual property protections. In the digital age, where intellectual property has become an increasingly important asset, the USMCA addressed the need to modernize trade rules to account for the rise of digital trade and e-commerce. The agreement introduced stronger protections for patents, trademarks, and copyrights, making it easier for U.S. businesses to protect their intellectual property across the three countries. It also included provisions to regulate cross-border data flows, ensuring that companies could send data freely between the U.S., Mexico, and Canada without facing excessive restrictions.

The USMCA also had provisions aimed at increasing U.S. agricultural exports. It expanded market access for American farmers in Canada and Mexico, particularly in areas like dairy, poultry, and wheat. These provisions were intended to benefit U.S. agricultural producers by opening up more markets for their goods, helping them compete with Canadian and Mexican producers who had previously had more favorable terms under NAFTA. However, some critics argued that these provisions were not enough to make up for the trade losses that occurred due to the tariffs imposed during the trade war with China, which had harmed U.S. farmers.

From a geopolitical perspective, the USMCA was also seen as a strategic move to counterbalance China's growing influence in the Western Hemisphere. By strengthening economic ties between the U.S., Mexico, and Canada, the agreement was intended to ensure that North America remained a competitive economic bloc in the face of China's rising economic power. In this context, the USMCA was not just about trade—it was also a tool for maintaining U.S. influence in the Americas.

While the USMCA brought about substantial changes to North American trade relations, it also sparked significant debate. Supporters hailed the agreement as a much-needed modernization of NAFTA that would benefit American workers, improve labor conditions, and strengthen the U.S. economy. Critics, however, argued that the deal did not go far enough in addressing issues like climate change and environmental protections, and that its overall economic impact would be limited. Nonetheless, the USMCA marked a pivotal moment in U.S. trade policy, reflecting Trump's broader goal of reshaping the global trade system to better serve American interests.

In conclusion, the USMCA was not merely a revision of NAFTA; it was a redefinition of trade deals, reflecting Trump's economic nationalism and his "America First" agenda. By focusing on domestic job creation, stronger labor standards, and updated intellectual property protections, the agreement aimed to shift the balance of trade in favor of the U.S. It also represented a broader trend of reshaping global trade deals to reflect a more protectionist and strategically driven approach. The success of the USMCA, like the broader impact of Trump's trade policies, remains a topic of ongoing debate, but it undeniably represents a significant shift in how the U.S. engages with its neighbors and the world.

America's Position in the World Trade Order

America's position in the world trade order has undergone significant transformations, particularly under the leadership of Donald Trump. Throughout much of the post-World War II era, the U.S. was a staunch advocate of free trade and multilateralism, helping to establish and sustain international economic institutions such as the World Trade Organization (WTO) and the International Monetary Fund (IMF). For decades, the U.S. leveraged its economic power to promote an open global trading system, believing that international trade would not only benefit individual nations but foster global peace and stability. However, under Trump's administration, America's approach to global trade shifted dramatically, as the U.S. adopted a more protectionist stance that prioritized national interests over international cooperation.

Trump's economic philosophy, which was built on the principles of economic nationalism, fundamentally challenged the global trade order. The "America First" agenda sought to reduce the U.S. trade deficit, protect American manufacturing jobs, and confront what Trump viewed as unfair trade practices by foreign nations. This shift was particularly evident in Trump's approach to trade agreements and his skepticism toward multilateral organizations. Under the administration, the U.S. withdrew from key international agreements such as the Trans-Pacific Partnership (TPP), a trade pact that aimed to deepen economic ties between the U.S. and several Asian nations. Trump's decision to pull out of the TPP was a clear signal that he favored bilateral trade deals that could be more directly tailored to America's economic interests, rather than multilateral agreements that involved compromises with other nations.

The most notable example of America's changing position in the global trade order was the trade war with China, which epitomized Trump's protectionist approach. The U.S. imposed tariffs on billions of dollars' worth of Chinese goods, citing unfair trade practices, intellectual property theft, and the trade imbalance between the two countries. While this confrontation resulted in significant disruptions in global trade and supply chains, it also marked a shift in the U.S. role within the global economic system. Trump's administration made it clear that the U.S. was no longer willing to passively accept global trade rules that were seen to disadvantage American workers and industries. Instead, the U.S. sought to impose its will on global trade by using tariffs and other protectionist tools as leverage in trade negotiations.

America's withdrawal from the Paris Climate Agreement and the World Health Organization (WHO), combined with the questioning of international trade institutions like the WTO, further highlighted Trump's departure from a multilateralist approach. Under the Trump administration, the U.S. sought to reduce its financial contributions to these global organizations and pushed for reforms that would prioritize American interests. The U.S. blocked the appointment of judges to the WTO's appellate body, essentially crippling the organization's ability to settle trade disputes effectively. This reflected Trump's broader skepticism toward international institutions that he believed had failed to serve U.S. interests. While the withdrawal from such organizations and the push for reforms were seen as detrimental to global cooperation by some critics, others viewed them as an attempt to recalibrate the global trade system in a way that would benefit America in the long run.

Despite these changes, the U.S. remained a central player in the world trade order, but its role had evolved. The U.S. continued to be the world's largest economy and a dominant force in global finance, technology, and innovation. American companies still played a crucial role in international trade, and the U.S. dollar remained the world's primary reserve currency. However, America's position was increasingly seen as one of rivalry and competition rather than cooperation. Countries like China, the European Union, and emerging markets took advantage of the U.S. retreat from multilateral agreements to strengthen their own economic ties and influence within global trade.

Under the Trump administration, the U.S. was also more focused on reducing its reliance on foreign goods and services, particularly from countries like China. The trade war and tariffs were intended to bring American manufacturing jobs back to the U.S. and reduce the trade imbalance. This approach to trade, however, was met with mixed results. While some industries benefited from the shift in supply chains, particularly those that had previously been outsourced to China, the tariffs also raised prices on consumer goods, causing inflationary pressures for American consumers. Additionally, the trade war led to a global slowdown in economic growth, as countries across the world adjusted to the new tariffs and trade restrictions imposed by the U.S.

In conclusion, under the leadership of Donald Trump, America's position in the world trade order shifted from one of global leadership and cooperation to one focused on national self-interest and economic nationalism. While the U.S. remained a central player in the global economy, its role was redefined by protectionist policies, trade wars, and a retreat from international institutions. Trump's approach to trade represented a sharp departure from the post-war consensus on global trade, marking a new era in which the U.S. sought to protect its own economic interests at the expense of multilateral cooperation. Whether this shift will have long-term benefits for the U.S. economy, or whether it will lead to a more fragmented global trade system, remains to be seen. However, the changes made during Trump's presidency will undoubtedly shape America's role in global trade for years to come.

Chapter 3
Tax Reform and Economic Growth

One of the hallmark achievements of Donald Trump's economic agenda was the implementation of significant tax reform, which he argued would stimulate economic growth, increase business investment, and provide relief to American workers. The Tax Cuts and Jobs Act (TCJA), passed in December 2017, marked the largest overhaul of the U.S. tax code in over three decades. Central to the reform was the dramatic reduction in the corporate tax rate, a move that Trump and his administration believed would make American businesses more competitive globally and encourage companies to repatriate profits and reinvest in the domestic economy. The tax cuts were seen as a critical component of the "America First" agenda, which aimed to create a more business-friendly environment that would fuel job creation and economic expansion.

In addition to the corporate tax cuts, the TCJA introduced a series of changes designed to benefit individual taxpayers. While corporate tax relief was the focal point of the reform, individual tax rates were also lowered, with the goal of boosting consumer spending. The standard deduction was nearly doubled, providing tax relief for millions of middle-class Americans. Trump's administration positioned these changes as a way to put more money back into the hands of consumers and stimulate demand, which in turn would drive economic growth. While the corporate tax cuts were permanent, the individual tax cuts were set to expire in 2025, sparking debates about the long-term sustainability of the reform.

Critics of the tax reform package, however, argued that the benefits were disproportionately skewed toward corporations and the wealthiest Americans. By significantly reducing the corporate tax rate, the reform primarily benefited large corporations, which saw a sharp increase in after-tax profits. Critics also raised concerns about the reform's impact on the federal deficit, as the reduction in tax revenues was not offset by corresponding cuts in government spending. Despite these criticisms, proponents of the reform maintained that the tax cuts would pay for themselves over time through higher economic growth, increased business investment, and job creation. As this chapter explores, the true impact of the TCJA on long-term economic growth remains a subject of ongoing debate, with some pointing to short-term gains while others question its long-term fiscal sustainability.

The Tax Cuts and Jobs Act

The Tax Cuts and Jobs Act (TCJA), signed into law by President Donald Trump on December 22, 2017, represented the largest overhaul of the U.S. tax code in over three decades. The reform aimed to stimulate economic growth, reduce the corporate tax burden, and provide tax relief to American individuals and businesses. It was a cornerstone of Trump's economic agenda, reflecting his belief that tax reductions would lead to greater business investment, job creation, and higher wages, while stimulating economic expansion across the nation. While the TCJA was celebrated by many for its potential to boost the economy, it also sparked significant controversy, with critics arguing that it disproportionately benefited the wealthiest Americans and increased the national deficit.

One of the most significant features of the TCJA was the drastic reduction in the corporate tax rate. Prior to the reform, the U.S. corporate tax rate stood at 35%, one of the highest in the developed world. The TCJA reduced this rate to 21%, bringing it more in line with other global economies. Proponents of the reform argued that this change would make American businesses more competitive internationally and encourage them to invest in domestic growth rather than moving operations overseas. The lowered corporate tax rate was seen as a way to incentivize companies to repatriate billions of dollars in profits that had been stashed abroad to avoid the high U.S. tax rate. The hope was that these tax savings would be used for investments in American workers, infrastructure, and innovation, which could lead to job creation and wage growth.

Another significant component of the TCJA was the reduction of tax rates for individuals. The law lowered the seven tax brackets that applied to individual income, reducing the tax burden for many American households. For example, the top individual tax rate was lowered from 39.6% to 37%, and lower-income earners saw a reduction in their tax rates as well. Additionally, the TCJA nearly doubled the standard deduction, which simplified tax filing for many Americans and reduced the taxable income for most taxpayers. For married couples filing jointly, the standard deduction increased from $12,700 to $24,000, offering substantial relief for middle-income families.

However, the TCJA also eliminated some long-standing tax deductions, such as the state and local tax (SALT) deduction, which allowed taxpayers to deduct state and local taxes from their federal tax bills. This move was particularly controversial in high-tax states like California, New York, and New Jersey, where many residents saw their overall tax burden increase as a result. The elimination of the SALT deduction was perceived as an effort to fund the broader tax cuts, but it disproportionately affected wealthier taxpayers in these states, contributing to the criticism that the TCJA favored the rich.

The TCJA also introduced a new provision aimed at encouraging U.S. companies to bring back profits held overseas. The reform included a one-time tax on overseas profits, allowing companies to repatriate these funds at a reduced tax rate of 15.5% for cash and 8% for non-cash assets. This was intended to incentivize companies to bring back some of the estimated $2.6 trillion held abroad, with hopes that it would be reinvested in the U.S. economy. Critics, however, argued that much of the repatriated money went to stock buybacks and dividends rather than new investments in the workforce or infrastructure.

Another major aspect of the TCJA was its provision for "pass-through" businesses—such as partnerships, sole proprietorships, and S corporations. These businesses, where the income is passed directly to the owners and taxed at individual rates, were given a new deduction. The law allowed pass-through businesses to deduct 20% of their income, which lowered the effective tax rate for many small business owners. However, the deduction had its limitations and faced criticism for benefiting wealthier individuals who owned large pass-through entities.

The TCJA also made temporary changes to the taxation of U.S. multinational corporations, shifting from a worldwide tax system to a territorial one. Under the new system, U.S. corporations were no longer taxed on foreign profits unless they were repatriated to the U.S. This shift was intended to make the U.S. tax system more competitive globally and to discourage the offshoring of profits.

Additionally, the TCJA introduced new provisions to encourage innovation and capital investment, such as the immediate expensing of certain capital investments, which allowed businesses to write off the costs of new equipment and infrastructure projects right away rather than over several years.

Despite these provisions, the TCJA faced strong criticism from opponents, particularly in regard to its long-term fiscal impact. The tax cuts, particularly for corporations and high-income individuals, were projected to increase the national deficit by trillions of dollars over the next decade. While proponents argued that the economic growth generated by the tax cuts would offset the lost revenue, critics contended that the cuts would disproportionately benefit the wealthiest Americans, widening income inequality and providing little lasting benefit to the middle and lower classes. The tax cuts were also criticized for being short-term measures, as many of the individual tax cuts were set to expire in 2025, while the corporate tax cuts were made permanent.

In conclusion, the Tax Cuts and Jobs Act was a landmark piece of legislation that redefined the U.S. tax landscape. By reducing corporate tax rates, cutting individual tax rates, and introducing new provisions aimed at encouraging business investment, the TCJA aimed to stimulate economic growth and create jobs. However, the reform also sparked significant controversy, particularly regarding its impact on the national deficit and its distribution of benefits. While it succeeded in lowering the tax burden for many Americans, critics argued that the tax cuts favored corporations and the wealthy, and that the long-term fiscal impact would be detrimental to the country's economic stability. The true legacy of the TCJA will depend on its long-term effects on the U.S. economy, and whether the promised growth materializes as anticipated.

Effects on Businesses and Individuals

The Tax Cuts and Jobs Act (TCJA) passed under President Donald Trump in December 2017 had far-reaching effects on both businesses and individuals in the United States. By reducing corporate tax rates, altering individual tax brackets, and introducing new incentives for business investment, the TCJA aimed to stimulate economic growth, boost job creation, and increase wages. While the law provided significant tax relief for many, its effects were not universally beneficial, leading to both praise and criticism for its perceived winners and losers.

Effects on Businesses

The most significant change brought about by the TCJA for businesses was the reduction in the corporate tax rate, which dropped from 35% to 21%. This marked one of the most dramatic corporate tax cuts in U.S. history. Proponents of the tax reform argued that this cut would make American businesses more competitive globally, especially in comparison to countries with lower corporate tax rates. The U.S. had long been seen as having one of the highest corporate tax rates among developed nations, which led many companies to seek tax advantages by moving operations overseas. By lowering the corporate tax rate, the TCJA aimed to reverse this trend, encouraging companies to keep jobs and capital investment within the U.S.

The TCJA also introduced provisions designed to encourage businesses to invest in their operations. One of the most significant of these was the ability for businesses to immediately expense (or "write off") the cost of certain capital investments, such as new equipment, machinery, and technology, rather than depreciating those assets over several years. This measure was intended to boost business investment, create jobs, and stimulate economic growth by making it easier for companies to upgrade their infrastructure and increase productivity. Furthermore, businesses were allowed to deduct up to 20% of income from pass-through entities like partnerships, LLCs, and S corporations, benefiting small business owners and entrepreneurs by lowering their effective tax rates.

However, the TCJA's benefits for businesses were not without controversy. Critics argued that the corporate tax cuts disproportionately favored large corporations, many of which already had the resources to make substantial investments, often resulting in stock buybacks and dividends rather than reinvestment in workforce expansion or new job creation. While companies did benefit from lower taxes, the promise of widespread wage increases or significant hiring was more limited. For instance, while companies like Apple and Walmart announced wage hikes and one-time bonuses, many other businesses used their tax savings to repurchase shares, which increased stock prices but did not directly benefit workers.

Effects on Individuals

For individuals, the TCJA lowered tax rates across multiple income brackets, providing tax relief for many American households. The law introduced a reduction in the seven tax brackets, with the top individual rate dropping from 39.6% to 37%. Additionally, the TCJA doubled the standard deduction, which greatly simplified the tax filing process for millions of Americans. For example, the standard deduction for married couples filing jointly increased from $12,700 to $24,000, significantly reducing the taxable income for many middle-class families.

While the individual tax cuts provided relief to many, they were not equally beneficial across all income groups. The TCJA's tax reductions were most significant for high-income earners, particularly those in the upper tax brackets. High-income households benefited from lower rates and additional tax breaks, such as the reduction in the Alternative Minimum Tax (AMT), which had previously limited deductions for high earners. Meanwhile, lower-income households saw less substantial benefits, as their tax cuts were smaller, and many of the changes were temporary. The individual tax cuts were designed to expire in 2025, leading critics to argue that the relief was not sustainable in the long term and would not provide lasting financial benefits for many working-class families.

Another significant change for individuals under the TCJA was the elimination of certain itemized deductions. The most notable of these was the limitation placed on the state and local tax (SALT) deduction. Prior to the TCJA, taxpayers could deduct state and local income, property, and sales taxes from their federal tax bills. The TCJA capped this deduction at $10,000, which disproportionately affected taxpayers in high-tax states like California, New York, and New Jersey. This change was particularly contentious, as it resulted in higher tax burdens for wealthy individuals in these states, who previously benefited from larger SALT deductions.

The elimination of personal exemptions under the TCJA was another area of concern for many individuals. Prior to the reform, taxpayers could claim a personal exemption for themselves, their spouses, and their dependents, which reduced taxable income. The TCJA eliminated these exemptions but increased the child tax credit, which helped to offset some of the lost benefits for families with children. However, critics argued that the loss of personal exemptions disproportionately hurt larger families or those with more dependents.

Overall, the effects of the Tax Cuts and Jobs Act on businesses and individuals were mixed. For businesses, the reduction in corporate tax rates and the incentives for investment were seen as positive for many large companies, leading to increased profits, stock buybacks, and some wage hikes. However, the benefits of the tax cuts were not always evenly distributed, and many small businesses or middle-income workers saw more modest benefits. For individuals, the TCJA provided substantial tax relief for many, particularly those in higher income brackets, but its effects were less pronounced for lower-income earners, and many of the tax cuts were temporary. Additionally, the changes to deductions, especially the SALT cap, led to increased taxes for many residents in high-tax states.

While the TCJA's impact on economic growth is still being debated, the law undoubtedly reshaped the tax landscape for both businesses and individuals. Whether the tax cuts will lead to sustained economic benefits or exacerbate income inequality remains a key question, with long-term effects that will continue to unfold in the years ahead.

Can Tax Cuts Fuel Sustainable Growth?

The idea that tax cuts can fuel sustainable economic growth has long been a subject of debate among economists and policymakers. Proponents of tax cuts, particularly supply-side economists, argue that reducing taxes—especially on businesses and high-income earners—can stimulate investment, job creation, and ultimately, lead to greater economic prosperity. This was the central argument behind the Tax Cuts and Jobs Act (TCJA) signed by President Donald Trump in 2017. The TCJA, which dramatically reduced corporate tax rates and offered individual tax cuts, was designed with the hope that lower taxes would stimulate growth by incentivizing businesses to invest in the U.S. economy, increasing wages, and encouraging more consumer spending. However, whether tax cuts can truly fuel sustainable growth remains a contentious question, with both short-term benefits and long-term challenges.

In the short term, tax cuts can certainly provide a boost to economic activity. When businesses pay less in taxes, they often have more capital to invest in infrastructure, technology, and labor. This can result in increased productivity, expansion of operations, and potentially higher wages for workers. Many businesses did indeed use the tax savings from the TCJA to invest in capital improvements, pay down debt, and, in some cases, raise employee wages or issue one-time bonuses. Moreover, the reduction in corporate tax rates aimed to make American businesses more competitive globally, helping to reverse the trend of companies moving operations overseas to take advantage of lower tax rates in other countries. For individual taxpayers, the immediate impact of lower tax rates increased disposable income, which in theory would encourage higher consumer spending and further stimulate the economy.

However, the long-term sustainability of this growth is less clear. While tax cuts can spur economic activity in the short term, they do not necessarily guarantee long-term growth, particularly if they lead to increased government debt. The TCJA, for example, is expected to add trillions of dollars to the federal deficit over the next decade. Critics argue that these large budget deficits could undermine the benefits of tax cuts, as the government will eventually need to raise revenue through other means, such as higher taxes or borrowing. This could place a strain on public finances, limiting the ability of the government to invest in other important areas like education, infrastructure, and healthcare. Moreover, if the tax cuts primarily benefit the wealthiest Americans or large corporations, the resulting increase in wealth inequality could dampen consumer spending and economic stability over time. Wealthier individuals tend to save rather than spend, meaning that the tax cuts may not generate as much consumer demand as hoped.

Another key consideration is the impact of tax cuts on innovation and entrepreneurship. While tax cuts may encourage businesses to invest in research and development or expand their operations, they do not automatically translate into innovation. Innovation requires not only capital investment but also a conducive environment—such as access to education, skilled labor, and a stable regulatory framework—that encourages creativity and entrepreneurship. Tax cuts alone do not address these fundamental drivers of long-term economic growth. Furthermore, tax cuts often come at the expense of government spending in other areas, which could undermine long-term investments in innovation and human capital development. Without sufficient investment in infrastructure, education, and healthcare, a tax-cut-driven economy may face limitations in terms of long-term growth potential.

Sustainable growth also depends on the structure and distribution of the tax cuts. If the cuts disproportionately benefit corporations and high-income individuals, they may lead to an increase in savings rather than spending, limiting their stimulative effect on the broader economy. Additionally, without corresponding investments in workforce development and education, the benefits of tax cuts may be unevenly distributed, potentially widening income inequality and leading to lower overall economic mobility. In such a scenario, even if the economy grows in the short term, it could become increasingly imbalanced, with the wealthiest individuals and corporations reaping the benefits while the middle and lower classes see little improvement in their economic well-being.

The overall effectiveness of tax cuts in fueling sustainable economic growth also depends on the broader economic context. In times of economic recession or stagnation, tax cuts may have a more significant impact by boosting demand and investment. However, during periods of economic expansion, the effects may be more muted, as businesses may not have as many immediate opportunities for reinvestment, and consumers may already be spending at high levels. In such cases, tax cuts may lead to inflationary pressures or create asset bubbles, which could ultimately undermine long-term economic stability.

In conclusion, while tax cuts can provide short-term economic benefits by stimulating investment, increasing disposable income, and making U.S. businesses more competitive, their ability to fuel sustainable growth is uncertain. The long-term impact depends on how the cuts are structured, how the resulting fiscal deficits are managed, and whether the broader economic environment supports innovation and human capital development. Tax cuts alone cannot guarantee sustainable economic growth; they must be part of a broader strategy that includes investments in infrastructure, education, and workforce development, along with policies that address inequality and ensure long-term fiscal health. Without these complementary efforts, tax cuts may only provide temporary relief, with long-term risks that could limit their effectiveness in achieving sustainable prosperity.

Chapter 4
The Role of Deregulation in Economic Expansion

Deregulation was a cornerstone of President Donald Trump's economic strategy, reflecting his belief that government intervention often stifled innovation, increased costs, and created barriers to business growth. From the very beginning of his presidency, Trump sought to reduce the regulatory burden on American businesses in a bid to foster a more competitive and efficient economic environment. By cutting red tape and rolling back policies enacted during the Obama administration, Trump aimed to unleash the full potential of the private sector, believing that less regulation would lead to increased investment, job creation, and overall economic expansion. This chapter explores the role of deregulation in Trump's economic vision, examining its impact on various industries and its broader effects on the economy.

One of the defining features of Trump's approach to deregulation was his goal of reducing the number of regulations governing businesses. In 2017, he signed an executive order requiring that for every new regulation introduced, two existing regulations must be eliminated. This directive was aimed at streamlining the regulatory process and eliminating what the administration viewed as unnecessary burdens on businesses, particularly in sectors like energy, banking, and healthcare. The idea was that by reducing the number of regulatory hurdles, businesses would have more freedom to operate, innovate, and expand, leading to higher productivity and job creation. This deregulatory push was met with support from industry groups, who argued that regulations often imposed excessive costs, particularly on small and medium-sized businesses, and that the government's role should be limited to ensuring a level playing field rather than dictating every aspect of business operations.

However, the effects of deregulation on economic expansion are complex and not without controversy. While many businesses welcomed the reduction in regulatory requirements, critics argued that it could lead to long-term negative consequences, particularly in sectors like environmental protection, financial services, and public health. Deregulation often involves loosening rules that were designed to protect consumers, workers, and the environment. The Trump administration's focus on energy independence, for example, led to the rollback of several environmental protections, such as the Clean Power Plan and restrictions on oil and gas drilling. While these moves were praised by the fossil fuel industry and those advocating for lower energy costs, environmental groups raised concerns about the potential long-term environmental damage and the undermining of efforts to combat climate change. As we delve into the role of deregulation in economic expansion, this chapter will examine both the positive and negative consequences of these policies and their lasting impact on the U.S. economy.

Unleashing the Private Sector

Unleashing the private sector was one of the central goals of President Donald Trump's economic policies. He firmly believed that a thriving, unencumbered private sector was the engine of economic growth, job creation, and innovation in America. Under his administration, the focus was on reducing the regulatory and tax burdens that, in his view, inhibited businesses from expanding and reaching their full potential. By creating an environment that was favorable to businesses, Trump aimed to encourage investment, increase competition, and drive the economy forward. This philosophy was encapsulated in his slogan "America First," which emphasized policies designed to empower American businesses and prioritize their interests in the global market.

One of the most significant ways that Trump sought to unleash the private sector was through deregulation. His administration made it a priority to reduce the number of federal regulations governing businesses, believing that the regulatory burden on companies—especially small businesses—was a major obstacle to growth. Trump issued an executive order that mandated for every new regulation introduced, two existing regulations must be eliminated. The goal was to simplify the regulatory environment and reduce red tape, which would make it easier for businesses to operate, invest, and hire. The deregulation agenda focused on several key industries, including energy, finance, and healthcare. In the energy sector, for example, Trump rolled back numerous environmental regulations, arguing that this would allow for greater energy production and lower costs for consumers. These moves were aimed at unlocking the full potential of the private sector by giving businesses the freedom to operate without what he deemed unnecessary governmental interference.

The tax reforms under the Tax Cuts and Jobs Act (TCJA) were another critical component of Trump's strategy to unleash the private sector. By cutting the corporate tax rate from 35% to 21%, Trump's administration aimed to make American businesses more competitive on the global stage. The TCJA also included provisions to allow businesses to immediately deduct the costs of certain capital investments, which would encourage them to reinvest profits into growth, innovation, and job creation. Proponents of these changes argued that by reducing the tax burden on businesses, they would have more capital to invest in expansion, research and development, and higher wages for employees. Lowering taxes was seen as a means of incentivizing businesses to remain in the U.S. or bring jobs back from overseas, particularly in industries like manufacturing, which had been heavily impacted by globalization and outsourcing.

Trump's deregulatory and tax policies were designed to create a favorable environment for entrepreneurship and business growth. By giving businesses greater freedom and fewer restrictions, he hoped to see an increase in private sector investment, higher levels of innovation, and more job creation. This approach resonated strongly with many business owners and entrepreneurs, particularly in industries that had faced heavy regulation, such as energy and banking. For example, the rollback of financial regulations implemented after the 2008 financial crisis, particularly the Dodd-Frank Act, was seen by some as a necessary step to allow banks and financial institutions to operate more freely and provide more loans and services to consumers. The private sector was seen as the key to driving economic expansion, with the idea being that businesses, when freed from excessive government interference, would naturally make decisions that would lead to broader prosperity.

However, the strategy of unleashing the private sector through deregulation and tax cuts was not without its critics. Opponents argued that the benefits of these policies were not evenly distributed and that they often favored large corporations and wealthy individuals, while providing limited relief to the middle class or small businesses. While large corporations saw significant tax savings and the ability to repurchase stocks, critics claimed that these benefits did not always translate into higher wages or increased hiring. Additionally, the focus on deregulation in certain sectors, such as the environment, raised concerns about the long-term sustainability of these policies. Critics warned that loosening regulations could lead to negative environmental consequences and economic instability, particularly in industries like banking, where a lack of oversight could lead to risky practices reminiscent of the pre-2008 financial crisis period.

Despite these criticisms, Trump's approach to unleashing the private sector was a cornerstone of his economic agenda. By cutting taxes, reducing regulations, and advocating for policies that favored business growth, his administration sought to create a climate where private enterprise could thrive. The overall impact of these policies is still debated, with some arguing that they led to increased business investment, stock market growth, and short-term job creation, while others believe that they contributed to growing income inequality and an unsustainable increase in the federal deficit. Nevertheless, Trump's emphasis on unleashing the private sector marked a significant shift in U.S. economic policy, reflecting his belief that a robust and dynamic private sector is essential to driving America's prosperity in the 21st century.

In conclusion, the goal of unleashing the private sector through deregulation and tax reform was central to Trump's vision for America's economic future. By reducing government intervention and lowering taxes, his administration aimed to foster an environment that encouraged business investment, job creation, and innovation. While these policies had clear benefits for many businesses, their long-term effectiveness and impact on economic inequality and fiscal health remain subjects of ongoing debate.

Ultimately, whether Trump's approach to unleashing the private sector contributed to sustainable economic growth or merely offered short-term gains will be determined by how the economy evolves in the years to come.

Impact on Industries: Energy, Banking, and Technology

The policies enacted during President Donald Trump's administration had profound impacts across various sectors of the U.S. economy, notably in energy, banking, and technology. His deregulatory agenda, tax reforms, and emphasis on energy independence reshaped these industries in significant ways. While some industries saw immediate growth and increased profitability, others faced challenges that raised questions about long-term sustainability, environmental impact, and financial stability. The administration's approach to these key sectors highlighted the central role of private enterprise in economic growth but also sparked intense debate about the balance between economic expansion and social responsibility.

Energy Industry

The energy sector was one of the most directly affected by Trump's policies. A central component of his economic agenda was to achieve energy independence for the U.S. and to reduce reliance on foreign energy sources. To accomplish this, Trump rolled back numerous environmental regulations, particularly those implemented during the Obama administration, which were aimed at reducing carbon emissions and promoting renewable energy sources. For example, Trump withdrew the U.S. from the Paris Climate Agreement, signaling a shift away from international commitments to address climate change. He also rolled back regulations like the Clean Power Plan, which aimed to reduce emissions from coal-fired power plants.

These deregulatory moves were designed to increase domestic energy production, particularly in the fossil fuel sectors. Trump's policies boosted the oil, natural gas, and coal industries, encouraging increased drilling, fracking, and mining activities. The U.S. became the world's top producer of oil and natural gas during his presidency, largely due to the expansion of hydraulic fracturing (fracking) in shale deposits. The lifting of restrictions on drilling in the Arctic and offshore areas also contributed to this surge in production. These policies were welcomed by energy companies and were credited with creating jobs in rural areas and providing energy security for the U.S. However, critics argued that these policies undermined environmental protections and contributed to long-term climate change risks. Environmental groups and many Democratic lawmakers warned that the unchecked expansion of fossil fuel production would exacerbate pollution, hinder the growth of renewable energy, and contribute to environmental degradation.

Banking Industry

Trump's policies also had significant implications for the banking industry, particularly with regard to financial regulation. One of his major objectives was to roll back regulations introduced after the 2008 financial crisis, such as those included in the Dodd-Frank Wall Street Reform and Consumer Protection Act. The Dodd-Frank Act was designed to prevent the risk-taking behavior that contributed to the financial crisis, imposing stricter oversight on banks and financial institutions. Trump and his administration viewed these regulations as overly burdensome and argued that they inhibited economic growth by limiting the ability of banks to lend and engage in certain types of financial activities.

In 2018, Trump signed the Economic Growth, Regulatory Relief, and Consumer Protection Act, which eased key provisions of Dodd-Frank. One of the most notable changes was raising the threshold for banks that were considered "too big to fail," from $50 billion in assets to $250 billion. This change meant that smaller banks faced less stringent regulatory scrutiny, which allowed them greater flexibility to make investments and take on more risk. Additionally, the law rolled back the Volcker Rule, which limited banks' ability to engage in proprietary trading (trading for their own profit). By easing these regulations, Trump aimed to foster greater lending activity, increase financial market liquidity, and boost economic growth.

However, the deregulation of the banking sector was met with criticism, particularly from consumer advocacy groups and those concerned about financial stability. Critics argued that loosening restrictions on banks could lead to increased risk-taking and potentially another financial crisis. There were concerns that without sufficient oversight, banks could once again engage in high-risk lending and speculative practices that could endanger the broader economy. Despite these concerns, the banking industry largely benefitted from the deregulation, with increased profits and a surge in lending activity, particularly in the commercial and housing sectors.

Technology Industry

The technology sector experienced a different set of challenges and opportunities during Trump's presidency. One of the major developments in this industry under the Trump administration was the push for reducing government intervention in business, which extended to technology and internet companies. The administration's deregulatory stance aimed to provide tech companies with greater autonomy in how they operate, especially with regard to antitrust enforcement and net neutrality. Trump's Federal Communications Commission (FCC), led by Chairman Ajit Pai, rolled back the net neutrality regulations put in place during the Obama administration, which prohibited internet service providers from throttling or blocking access to specific websites. By dismantling these rules, the administration argued that companies would have greater incentives to invest in broadband infrastructure, leading to better service and more competition. However, critics believed that without net neutrality protections, consumers could face higher prices and limited access to online content.

Trump's trade policies also impacted the tech industry, particularly in its relationship with China. The U.S. trade war with China had significant ramifications for tech companies that relied on Chinese manufacturing and markets. China is a major producer of electronics and a key market for American tech products, so tariffs imposed on Chinese goods, along with restrictions on Chinese companies like Huawei, disrupted supply chains and business operations for U.S. tech giants. While Trump's administration argued that these actions were necessary to protect U.S. intellectual property and national security, they placed considerable pressure on American tech companies, many of which rely on Chinese suppliers for components like semiconductors.

Moreover, the administration's stance on immigration and foreign labor affected the technology sector, which has long depended on highly skilled workers from abroad. Trump's more restrictive immigration policies, including limitations on H-1B visas, made it more difficult for tech companies to recruit talent from other countries, potentially leading to labor shortages in critical fields like software development and data science.

In conclusion, Trump's policies had varying impacts on the energy, banking, and technology industries. In energy, deregulation led to increased fossil fuel production but raised environmental concerns. In banking, the rollback of Dodd-Frank regulations helped spur lending but raised fears of financial instability. In technology, deregulation and trade policies presented both opportunities and challenges, especially in terms of global supply chains, labor shortages, and government oversight. While these policies were designed to unleash the potential of the private sector and stimulate growth, their long-term effects on sustainability, stability, and innovation remain a subject of debate.

Balancing Regulation and Market Freedom

The debate over balancing regulation and market freedom is at the heart of modern economic policy discussions. On one side, proponents of deregulation argue that markets thrive best when businesses are allowed to operate with minimal government intervention. They contend that regulations can stifle innovation, slow down economic growth, and increase costs for businesses and consumers. On the other hand, advocates of regulation assert that some level of oversight is necessary to protect consumers, the environment, workers, and the broader economy from the excesses and negative externalities that unregulated markets can produce. Achieving the right balance between these two forces is a complex challenge that requires careful consideration of the economic, social, and environmental consequences of each regulatory decision.

During President Donald Trump's administration, the focus was firmly on deregulation, driven by the belief that reducing the regulatory burden would unleash economic growth, increase job creation, and promote innovation. The Trump administration set ambitious goals for reducing the number of regulations on businesses. One of the most notable policies was the executive order requiring that for every new regulation introduced, two existing regulations must be eliminated. This was aimed at simplifying the regulatory environment and reducing what the administration viewed as unnecessary and burdensome rules that hindered business operations. Key sectors, including energy, finance, and healthcare, saw significant deregulatory efforts. The rollback of environmental regulations, for example, aimed to reduce the cost of energy production, especially for the oil, gas, and coal industries, which benefitted from fewer restrictions on drilling, emissions, and pollution controls. The logic was that lowering these costs would incentivize businesses to invest more in expansion and create jobs, leading to overall economic growth.

However, while deregulation was intended to boost business activity, critics of this approach raised important concerns about the potential risks of reducing government oversight. One key criticism was that removing regulations, particularly those designed to protect the environment, consumers, and workers, could lead to a range of negative consequences. For instance, the rollback of regulations aimed at controlling carbon emissions could exacerbate climate change and pollution, creating long-term environmental and public health costs. Similarly, the dismantling of financial regulations, such as those introduced after the 2008 financial crisis, raised concerns about the potential for risky lending practices and another financial meltdown. Critics argued that excessive deregulation could lead to market failures, where businesses engage in harmful practices or take excessive risks without accountability, ultimately causing greater harm to the economy and society than the regulations sought to prevent.

The question, therefore, becomes not whether regulation is good or bad, but how to strike a balance that promotes market freedom while safeguarding public interests. One of the challenges in achieving this balance is determining which regulations are necessary and which ones are overly restrictive. For example, many supporters of deregulation argue that environmental regulations, while important, should not unnecessarily restrict economic activity. They suggest that environmental protection could be achieved through market-based mechanisms, such as carbon taxes or cap-and-trade systems, that incentivize businesses to reduce pollution without mandating specific practices. Similarly, in the banking sector, regulations like the Dodd-Frank Act were put in place to prevent risky practices that led to the 2008 financial crisis. However, proponents of deregulation argued that these rules were too restrictive and prevented banks from engaging in normal lending activities, which, in their view, hindered economic recovery. The challenge lies in finding regulations that protect consumers and the environment without imposing excessive burdens on businesses.

One way to achieve a more effective balance is through targeted, evidence-based regulation. Rather than adopting a blanket approach that either deregulates or over-regulates entire industries, policymakers can focus on the specific risks posed by different sectors and tailor regulations to address those risks. For example, in the case of financial regulation, lawmakers could create a framework that allows for greater flexibility in banking practices but includes strong safeguards to ensure that institutions do not engage in overly risky or predatory behavior. In the energy sector, rather than eliminating environmental regulations entirely, policymakers could focus on creating incentives for businesses to adopt cleaner technologies or improve efficiency, thus aligning environmental goals with economic incentives.

Moreover, a well-regulated market can also promote competition and consumer welfare. In many industries, regulations serve to protect consumers from unfair practices, deceptive advertising, or unsafe products. In the tech industry, for example, antitrust laws are designed to prevent monopolies and promote competition, ensuring that consumers have access to a variety of goods and services at fair prices. A free market without regulation can lead to situations where large corporations dominate the market, reducing competition and ultimately harming consumers. Similarly, financial regulations can ensure that consumers are protected from exploitative lending practices and that banks remain solvent and trustworthy.

Ultimately, the challenge is not simply reducing regulations or increasing them, but ensuring that regulations are effective, targeted, and designed to address specific market failures or risks. While deregulation can spur economic growth in the short term, it must be tempered with safeguards to ensure that market freedom does not come at the expense of long-term stability, fairness, and sustainability. By focusing on evidence-based policies and fostering a regulatory environment that promotes both economic growth and public welfare, it is possible to achieve a balance that maximizes the benefits of a free market while minimizing its potential harms.

Chapter 5
The Future of American Jobs in a Globalized Economy

The future of American jobs in a globalized economy is one of the most pressing challenges facing the United States today. With the rapid advancements in technology, shifting trade dynamics, and changing labor markets, the landscape of employment is evolving faster than ever before. During the Trump administration, the focus was heavily placed on bringing back jobs that had been outsourced or lost to automation, especially in traditional industries like manufacturing. This vision was encapsulated by the "America First" agenda, which sought to renegotiate trade deals, reduce corporate tax burdens, and implement protectionist policies that would, in theory, revitalize the American workforce. However, the question remains: can the U.S. really return to a world where manufacturing and labor-intensive jobs drive the economy, or must it adapt to the new reality of a globally interconnected, technology-driven workforce?

Globalization has led to increased competition and the outsourcing of many American jobs, particularly in the manufacturing sector, to countries with lower labor costs. This trend was accelerated by the rise of China and other emerging economies, which, over the past few decades, have become major players in global supply chains. While this global interconnectedness has benefitted many U.S. consumers by lowering prices and increasing access to goods, it has also contributed to the erosion of domestic manufacturing jobs. The U.S. has seen significant declines in industries like textiles, automotive production, and electronics assembly. For many workers in these sectors, particularly in Rust Belt regions, the loss of these jobs has created deep economic and social challenges. Trump's administration promised to reverse this trend by encouraging companies to bring jobs back to the U.S. through tax cuts, tariffs, and trade renegotiations. However, the broader question remains: can the U.S. truly re-establish its past industrial dominance in a world where production costs are central to global competition?

As automation and artificial intelligence (AI) continue to advance, the nature of work itself is shifting. Many jobs that were once performed by humans are increasingly being automated, particularly in industries like manufacturing, retail, and logistics. In some ways, automation and AI could serve as catalysts for higher productivity and innovation, but they also present a challenge to the traditional workforce. As jobs become more technologically advanced, workers must adapt by acquiring new skills and competencies. The question becomes whether the U.S. education system and workforce training programs are equipped to meet this challenge. While some jobs are being lost to technology, others are being created in fields like data science, cybersecurity, and renewable energy. The future of American jobs, therefore, depends not only on policies to bring manufacturing jobs back but also on how effectively the workforce can transition to new, technology-driven roles in a rapidly changing economy. This chapter will explore the complexities of these shifts and the policies and strategies needed to ensure that American workers can thrive in a globalized, tech-driven economy.

Revitalizing Manufacturing: Jobs vs. Automation

The revitalization of American manufacturing has been a central focus of economic policy, especially under the Trump administration, which promised to bring back jobs lost to outsourcing and automation. Manufacturing, once a key driver of economic prosperity and job creation in the U.S., has been in decline for decades. While the loss of jobs to outsourcing was one significant factor, the rise of automation and technology-driven manufacturing has presented new challenges for the future of the sector. As the global economy continues to evolve, the debate surrounding jobs versus automation has become increasingly complex. Can manufacturing in the U.S. be revitalized through human labor, or will automation ultimately dominate, changing the nature of work in the industry?

For much of the 20th century, the manufacturing sector provided millions of well-paying jobs in the United States, especially in industries like steel, automotive, and textiles. However, in recent decades, many of these jobs were outsourced to countries with lower labor costs, primarily in Asia. This outsourcing, driven by globalization, resulted in significant job losses in the U.S., particularly in industrial regions such as the Rust Belt. In response, policymakers have focused on bringing back these jobs, emphasizing the importance of manufacturing to the American economy. President Trump, for instance, repeatedly pledged to "bring back manufacturing" through policies aimed at reshoring jobs, such as renegotiating trade deals and imposing tariffs on foreign goods. The hope was that by creating more favorable conditions for U.S. companies, manufacturing jobs would return and the U.S. economy would regain its industrial strength.

However, even as some jobs have been brought back to the U.S., a critical factor in the future of manufacturing is the role of automation. Automation and robotics have already transformed manufacturing processes, reducing the need for manual labor in many sectors. Machines now perform tasks that were once done by humans, such as assembly, packaging, and quality control. The impact of automation is particularly evident in industries like automotive manufacturing, where robots perform highly precise and repetitive tasks more efficiently than human workers. The result is a significant reduction in the number of workers needed to run production lines, even as manufacturing output increases. Automation has improved productivity and allowed U.S. manufacturers to remain competitive in a global market, but it has also raised concerns about the displacement of workers, particularly in low-skill, low-wage jobs.

The key challenge facing the U.S. manufacturing sector today is finding the balance between revitalizing jobs and embracing automation. On the one hand, automation has the potential to improve efficiency and quality, reduce costs, and drive innovation. For example, the rise of 3D printing, AI-driven design, and automated supply chains allows companies to produce goods faster and with fewer defects. Additionally, automation can help manufacturers compete in global markets, where countries with lower labor costs often have a competitive advantage. However, these technological advancements come at the cost of jobs, especially for workers who lack the skills to operate and manage sophisticated machines.

To revitalize manufacturing while addressing the impact of automation on jobs, it is essential to focus on workforce development and education. As automation continues to advance, the demand for skilled workers who can operate, program, and maintain machines has risen. Manufacturing workers today need to be well-versed in technology, and the sector is increasingly looking for employees with expertise in robotics, programming, and data analysis. For workers displaced by automation, retraining and reskilling programs are critical to help them transition to new roles in a more tech-driven economy. Policymakers, educational institutions, and businesses must collaborate to provide workers with the skills needed to thrive in this new landscape. By investing in education and training, the U.S. can ensure that workers are not left behind as manufacturing becomes more automated.

At the same time, there are still opportunities for labor in manufacturing, even as automation plays a larger role. While automation can replace many manual tasks, it also creates jobs in the design, operation, and maintenance of the technologies used in production. Additionally, as manufacturers invest in advanced manufacturing processes like robotics and AI, new industries and job opportunities will emerge. However, these jobs will require higher skill levels and education than traditional manufacturing jobs. The future of American manufacturing will not solely be about restoring the jobs lost to outsourcing, but about adapting to the technological changes that have reshaped the sector.

In conclusion, revitalizing U.S. manufacturing involves more than just bringing back old jobs; it requires a comprehensive approach that balances the benefits of automation with the need for a skilled workforce. While automation has undeniably reduced the number of low-skill manufacturing jobs, it has also opened up new opportunities for workers with the right skills. The key to success will be ensuring that workers are not left behind as the sector modernizes. By focusing on education, training, and workforce development, the

U.S. can maintain its manufacturing competitiveness while ensuring that workers can adapt to the changing demands of the industry.

The Gig Economy and Freelance Workforce

The gig economy, characterized by short-term contracts or freelance work rather than permanent, full-time employment, has become an increasingly significant part of the global labor market, including in the United States. Over the past decade, technological advances, particularly in digital platforms and online marketplaces, have facilitated the rapid growth of gig and freelance work. Whether it's driving for ride-sharing services, delivering food, or offering specialized freelance skills like graphic design and writing, the gig economy has become a prominent avenue for employment, offering flexibility and independence. While the gig economy offers many opportunities for workers and businesses alike, it also raises important questions about job security, benefits, and the future of work.

One of the primary attractions of the gig economy is its flexibility. Workers have the freedom to choose when, where, and how much they work, which allows them to better balance their personal and professional lives. For many, this flexibility is especially appealing as it offers the ability to tailor their working hours around other commitments, such as caring for children, pursuing other passions, or simply avoiding the typical 9-to-5 grind. Freelance workers, who make up a significant portion of the gig economy, can take on multiple clients or projects simultaneously, allowing them to diversify their income streams and explore different areas of work. This level of autonomy has made gig work particularly attractive to younger generations, such as millennials and Gen Z, who value work-life balance and seek greater control over their professional lives.

For businesses, the gig economy presents a significant opportunity to tap into a flexible, on-demand labor force. Companies can hire freelancers or gig workers for specific tasks or projects without the overhead costs associated with full-time employees. This allows businesses to scale their workforce up or down quickly depending on demand, making it a highly efficient way to manage labor costs. For example, tech companies, in particular, have embraced freelance and contract-based work for project-specific tasks like software development, marketing campaigns, and design work. Gig workers can often be hired for specialized skills that may not be needed on a full-time basis, providing businesses with access to high-quality talent without long-term commitments. The rise of online platforms like Upwork, Fiverr, and Freelancer has further facilitated this trend, making it easier than ever for businesses to find, hire, and manage freelance workers globally.

However, while the gig economy offers numerous advantages, it also raises significant challenges, particularly in terms of worker protections. Gig workers are typically classified as independent contractors, meaning they are not entitled to the same benefits and protections as traditional employees. This includes access to healthcare, retirement savings plans, paid leave, and unemployment benefits. Without these safety nets, gig workers often face financial instability, particularly in times of economic downturn or when they experience a gap between gigs. Many gig workers must shoulder the responsibility of managing their own taxes, healthcare, and insurance, which can be difficult, especially for those who rely on gig work as their primary income source.

The issue of job security is another concern in the gig economy. While the flexibility of gig work can be appealing, it also means that workers often face inconsistent income. Gig workers may not know from week to week how much they will earn, and without job security or guaranteed hours, they are left vulnerable to market fluctuations or shifts in demand. In some industries, like transportation or delivery, workers can experience sharp declines in earnings due to factors such as seasonal demand or increased competition. For example, ride-sharing drivers may see their earnings decrease if there is an oversupply of drivers in their area, leading to fewer rides and lower pay.

As the gig economy continues to grow, policymakers have begun to grapple with how to provide better protections for gig workers while maintaining the flexibility that makes this model so attractive. Some states and countries have taken steps to extend certain rights to gig workers, such as guaranteeing minimum wage or offering paid sick leave. In California, the passage of Assembly Bill 5 (AB5) aimed to classify certain gig workers as employees rather than independent contractors, granting them benefits like unemployment insurance and workers' compensation. However, this move has been controversial, as it could potentially limit the flexibility that many gig workers value and create higher costs for businesses that rely on a freelance workforce.

Despite these challenges, the gig economy continues to expand, fueled by technological advancements and changing attitudes toward work. As more workers turn to freelance and contract work, it is likely that businesses will increasingly adapt to a labor force that prioritizes flexibility and autonomy. To ensure the long-term success of the gig economy, it will be necessary to strike a balance between the freedom and flexibility that gig work offers and the protections that workers need to thrive. This could involve developing new models for worker classification, expanding access to benefits, and creating innovative solutions to support gig workers in times of financial hardship.

In conclusion, the gig economy and freelance workforce have reshaped the way people work and how businesses operate. Offering flexibility, autonomy, and access to specialized talent, the gig economy has become an essential part of the modern labor market. However, as this sector continues to grow, addressing the challenges of job security, benefits, and worker protections will be crucial to ensuring that the gig economy can sustain its growth while supporting the well-being of its workers.

Education and Skills Development for the Future

As the global economy continues to evolve, the demand for new skills and knowledge is rapidly changing. Technological advancements, particularly in automation, artificial intelligence (AI), data analytics, and renewable energy, are reshaping the job market and creating opportunities in fields that were unimaginable just a few decades ago. To keep pace with these shifts, education and skills development must be reimagined to equip future generations with the tools they need to thrive in an increasingly complex and interconnected world. This requires not only adapting current education systems but also embracing new models of lifelong learning that provide workers with the flexibility and resources to develop the skills needed throughout their careers.

One of the most pressing challenges in education today is ensuring that students are prepared for the jobs of the future. The rapid pace of technological change means that many traditional jobs are becoming obsolete, while entirely new professions are emerging. For example, fields like cybersecurity, AI, machine learning, and digital marketing did not exist in their current form just a decade ago. As automation and robotics continue to replace routine tasks in industries like manufacturing, transportation, and retail, the demand for highly skilled workers in technology-driven sectors is expected to grow exponentially. This shift presents a challenge for traditional education systems, which often emphasize subjects like literature, history, and the arts, without giving equal attention to science, technology, engineering, and mathematics (STEM) fields. To address this gap, there needs to be a stronger focus on STEM education at all levels, from primary through higher education.

Moreover, education systems must evolve to place greater emphasis on skills that are not only technical but also transferable across industries. Critical thinking, problem-solving, creativity, emotional intelligence, and adaptability are increasingly recognized as essential for success in the modern workforce. These skills enable individuals to navigate the complexities of a rapidly changing job market, where job roles and responsibilities are continually shifting. To foster these skills, education systems should prioritize project-based learning, real-world applications, and collaboration, providing students with opportunities to work on interdisciplinary projects that challenge their thinking and require them to solve problems creatively. Additionally, fostering an entrepreneurial mindset—teaching students to innovate and embrace risk—can prepare them for the ever-changing economic landscape.

In addition to restructuring traditional education pathways, skills development must also include a robust system of lifelong learning. As industries evolve and new technologies emerge, workers will need to constantly update their skills to remain relevant in the job market. Lifelong learning allows individuals to acquire new competencies at any stage of their careers, providing them with the flexibility to transition between industries and roles. Governments, businesses, and educational institutions all have a role to play in promoting and facilitating lifelong learning. For example, many countries have already implemented or are exploring policies that provide funding or incentives for adult learners to pursue further education or specialized training. Corporate partnerships with universities and vocational schools can create pathways for workers to gain industry-specific certifications, ensuring that their skills remain in demand.

The role of technology itself in education is also critical to the future of skills development. Online learning platforms, such as Coursera, Udacity, and edX, are already democratizing education, making high-quality learning opportunities accessible to people worldwide, regardless of location or background. These platforms offer courses on a variety of subjects, from computer programming to digital marketing, and allow learners to gain certifications that are recognized by employers. Moreover, technologies like AI and machine learning are being incorporated into educational tools, providing personalized learning experiences that adapt to individual needs and progress. Virtual and augmented reality (VR/AR) are also emerging as powerful tools for immersive learning, particularly in fields like healthcare, engineering, and design. These technologies enable students to practice skills in a safe, controlled environment, improving their understanding and confidence before they apply those skills in the real world.

To prepare the workforce for the future, it is essential that we bridge the gap between formal education and the skills required by employers. One way to do this is by strengthening the connection between educational institutions and industry leaders. Apprenticeships, internships, and co-op programs provide students with hands-on experience in the workforce, allowing them to apply their knowledge and gain insights into what is expected in specific fields. By working closely with industries, educational institutions can ensure that curricula are aligned with the needs of the job market, offering programs that teach both hard and soft skills. Additionally, businesses can offer employees opportunities to learn on the job, creating a culture of continuous development within organizations.

Finally, education and skills development for the future must be inclusive. The benefits of technological advancement and economic growth should be available to all, regardless of socioeconomic background, race, or geographic location. Expanding access to quality education and training programs is essential to closing the skills gap and ensuring that all individuals have an equal opportunity to succeed. This includes investing in underserved communities, providing financial support for low-income students, and offering resources for adult learners who are returning to education later in life. By promoting inclusivity, we can create a more equitable future of work, where individuals from diverse backgrounds have the opportunity to thrive in an ever-evolving economy.

In conclusion, education and skills development are at the heart of preparing for the future of work. To succeed in the globalized, technology-driven economy, individuals must be equipped with both technical skills and transferable competencies that enable them to adapt to change. This requires a transformation of traditional education systems, a greater emphasis on lifelong learning, and the integration of technology to provide accessible, personalized learning experiences. With the right investments and policies, we can build a workforce that is not only capable of thriving in the future but also resilient in the face of ongoing change.

Chapter 6
Infrastructure Investment and Economic Prosperity

Infrastructure investment plays a pivotal role in fostering long-term economic prosperity, as it directly affects the efficiency and productivity of an economy. From roads and bridges to telecommunications networks and energy systems, a country's infrastructure forms the backbone of its economy. For businesses, efficient infrastructure reduces costs, improves supply chain management, and enhances connectivity, while for individuals, it improves access to jobs, education, and healthcare. During the Trump administration, infrastructure investment was frequently touted as a key driver for economic growth and job creation. Trump's "America First" agenda emphasized revitalizing America's aging infrastructure, which he argued had become a barrier to economic growth, making it more difficult for U.S. businesses to compete globally. As the U.S. navigates the complexities of the 21st century, it is clear that strategic infrastructure investment is crucial to maintaining and accelerating economic prosperity.

Despite the undeniable importance of infrastructure, the U.S. has faced a significant challenge in maintaining and upgrading its systems, which are often outdated and in disrepair. The American Society of Civil Engineers (ASCE) regularly issues reports on the state of U.S. infrastructure, and in its 2017 report, the country received a grade of D+ for its infrastructure quality, signaling a pressing need for improvements. Trump's infrastructure plan, however, was met with mixed reactions. While the administration proposed a $1.5 trillion infrastructure investment plan, it relied heavily on private-sector involvement and state-level funding, rather than solely federal investment. Critics argued that this approach would lead to insufficient funding, particularly in poorer areas that may lack the financial resources to participate in such public-private partnerships. Nevertheless, the central premise was clear: by investing in infrastructure, the government could stimulate the economy, create jobs, and enhance the overall competitiveness of the U.S. economy.

Long-term economic prosperity is deeply connected to robust and modern infrastructure systems, which facilitate smoother economic transactions and promote higher living standards. Modernizing infrastructure, particularly through the integration of technology and green energy solutions, can have far-reaching effects, including the creation of sustainable jobs and boosting innovation. This chapter will explore the relationship between infrastructure investment and economic growth, examining how strategic investments in transportation, energy, and digital connectivity can support productivity, reduce inefficiencies, and ultimately elevate the prosperity of the nation. By evaluating the successes and challenges of infrastructure initiatives in recent years, we can better understand how targeted investments can shape the economic trajectory of the future.

The Plan for Rebuilding America's Infrastructure

The state of America's infrastructure has long been a source of concern for both policymakers and business leaders. As the U.S. economy continues to grow, the need for modern, efficient, and sustainable infrastructure has become increasingly urgent. Aging roads, bridges, public transit systems, energy grids, and outdated communication networks create significant bottlenecks that hinder economic productivity, increase costs, and reduce quality of life. Addressing these challenges is essential to maintaining America's global competitiveness. During the Trump administration, the rebuilding of America's infrastructure was framed as one of the most critical aspects of the broader economic agenda. Trump's plan to revitalize the nation's infrastructure focused on leveraging both federal and private sector investment to improve the country's core systems, ultimately driving economic growth, job creation, and long-term prosperity.

Trump's infrastructure proposal, introduced in early 2018, outlined a vision for rebuilding and modernizing U.S. infrastructure, calling for a $1.5 trillion investment in areas such as transportation, energy, and broadband expansion. The administration's plan was unique in that it sought to shift much of the responsibility for funding to state and local governments as well as the private sector, rather than relying solely on federal funding. The plan proposed that the federal government provide $200 billion in direct grants and incentives, with the remaining funds to be raised through state-level contributions and private investments. This public-private partnership (PPP) approach was designed to stimulate additional investment from the private sector, encouraging companies to fund and manage specific infrastructure projects. While the plan aimed to modernize infrastructure quickly, it was met with criticism for relying too heavily on state and local governments to shoulder the burden, especially in poorer regions that may not have the resources to engage in such partnerships.

A major focus of the plan was improving the nation's transportation infrastructure. The U.S. has an extensive network of roads and highways, but many of these are aging and in poor condition, with a significant number of bridges and roads requiring immediate repairs. The Trump administration proposed investing in highways, bridges, and roads to reduce congestion, improve safety, and increase efficiency in the movement of goods and people. This was viewed as a crucial step in boosting productivity and reducing costs for businesses that rely on these systems for supply chains and logistics. The proposal also called for substantial investments in public transit systems, particularly in urban areas where congestion and outdated infrastructure are significant issues. In addition to roads and public transit, Trump's plan included modernizing airports and ports to improve international trade and ensure that the U.S. remains competitive in the global economy.

Another key component of the infrastructure plan was addressing the country's energy infrastructure. The U.S. energy grid is under increasing strain due to rising demand, extreme weather events, and outdated systems that were not designed to handle renewable energy sources. The Trump administration sought to modernize the grid to ensure it could meet future energy demands, including the integration of more renewable energy sources such as solar and wind. In addition, Trump's plan proposed expanding natural gas pipelines, improving energy storage capabilities, and upgrading electricity transmission systems to ensure a more reliable, efficient, and resilient energy network. Although the administration's emphasis on fossil fuels, such as natural gas, faced criticism from environmental groups, the plan aimed to ensure that the U.S. had a more secure and sustainable energy infrastructure.

Broadband infrastructure was also a major focus of Trump's infrastructure initiative. In many rural areas, access to high-speed internet remains limited, creating barriers to education, healthcare, and economic opportunities. Trump's plan called for expanding broadband access to underserved communities, ensuring that every American had access to fast and reliable internet. This effort was seen as a critical step in supporting economic growth, particularly in rural areas, and fostering greater equality of opportunity. The expansion of broadband infrastructure was also seen as a means to promote innovation, entrepreneurship, and digital inclusion, helping to close the digital divide in America.

However, the plan faced significant challenges in terms of funding and political support. While the administration's vision for rebuilding America's infrastructure was bold, the reliance on state and local governments to fund a substantial portion of the investment raised concerns, particularly in regions with limited resources. Critics argued that such an approach would disproportionately benefit wealthier areas, leaving poorer communities without the means to engage in these partnerships. Furthermore, despite the calls for bipartisan support, the plan faced pushback from Democrats, who argued that the proposal lacked sufficient investment in green energy infrastructure and environmental protections. The plan was also criticized for not providing a clear timeline or specific targets for how projects would be prioritized or implemented.

Despite these obstacles, the infrastructure plan highlighted the crucial need for investment in America's physical and digital infrastructure to maintain economic growth, competitiveness, and quality of life. In the long term, infrastructure investment offers substantial returns in terms of job creation, improved efficiency, and economic productivity. While the Trump administration's approach was met with mixed reviews, the conversation it sparked around the need to modernize infrastructure continues to influence policy discussions at both the federal and state levels.

In conclusion, rebuilding America's infrastructure is critical to the nation's long-term economic prosperity. The Trump administration's $1.5 trillion infrastructure plan emphasized the importance of public-private partnerships, with a focus on revitalizing transportation, energy, and broadband systems. While the plan's approach and funding model raised questions and faced opposition, it brought attention to the pressing need for modern, resilient infrastructure. As America continues to navigate the complexities of the 21st century economy, investing in infrastructure will remain a central strategy to support growth, create jobs, and ensure the competitiveness of U.S. industries on the global stage.

Public-Private Partnerships: A New Economic Model

Public-Private Partnerships (PPPs) have become an increasingly popular economic model as governments around the world seek innovative solutions to address infrastructure deficits, promote economic development, and reduce the financial burden on taxpayers. By combining the strengths of both the public and private sectors, PPPs can deliver large-scale projects more efficiently, leveraging private sector expertise, innovation, and funding while still ensuring that the public interest is prioritized. This collaborative approach has the potential to transform how critical public infrastructure is developed and maintained, especially in times of limited government budgets and rising demands for services. However, while PPPs offer significant benefits, they also come with their own set of challenges and risks.

At the heart of a PPP is the sharing of responsibilities and resources between the public and private sectors. In traditional public sector projects, the government is typically responsible for both funding and overseeing the construction and operation of infrastructure. In contrast, a PPP involves private companies financing, designing, building, and often operating public infrastructure projects, such as roads, bridges, hospitals, schools, and energy facilities. In return for their investment, private partners usually receive revenue through user fees, long-term contracts, or a combination of public payments and private revenues, which can provide a return on their investment. This allows the government to undertake large projects without shouldering the full financial burden upfront, making it possible to address pressing infrastructure needs without immediately raising taxes or increasing debt.

One of the key advantages of PPPs is the potential for increased efficiency and innovation. Private companies often bring specialized expertise and advanced technologies to the table, allowing for more streamlined project management, faster completion times, and higher quality standards. In infrastructure projects, where delays and cost overruns can be significant issues, the private sector's drive for profit and efficiency can lead to better outcomes. Additionally, the competitive bidding process for PPP contracts often results in lower costs for taxpayers, as companies strive to offer the best value for the project. This combination of efficiency and cost-effectiveness is particularly important for governments that are constrained by budgetary limitations but still need to modernize infrastructure to meet the demands of a growing population and economy.

Another benefit of PPPs is the opportunity for risk-sharing between the public and private sectors. In many traditional public sector projects, governments bear the full financial and operational risk of delivering infrastructure. With PPPs, however, the risks are more evenly distributed. For example, if a project experiences cost overruns or delays, the private partner may be required to absorb those additional costs, rather than passing them onto taxpayers. This arrangement helps align the incentives of both parties: the government gets access to high-quality infrastructure, and the private sector is incentivized to complete the project on time and within budget. Additionally, because private companies typically have long-term performance incentives tied to the operation and maintenance of infrastructure, there is an added focus on the long-term sustainability and efficiency of the project.

Despite these advantages, PPPs are not without their challenges and risks. One of the primary concerns is the complexity of these arrangements. PPPs require detailed contracts that clearly define the roles and responsibilities of each party, the expected returns for the private sector, and the performance metrics that must be met. Negotiating these contracts can be time-consuming and expensive, and if not carefully structured, they can result in disputes, legal challenges, or unanticipated costs. Furthermore, the long-term nature of PPP agreements (which can last 20-30 years or more) means that governments must commit to providing consistent payments over an extended period, which can sometimes strain public finances, particularly if economic conditions change or projected revenues do not materialize.

Another issue with PPPs is the risk of privatization, particularly when it comes to public services. In some cases, privatizing key infrastructure or services, such as water supply or toll roads, can lead to higher costs for consumers, as private companies seek to maximize profits. The need to balance private sector profits with public service goals is a delicate issue, and in some cases, private partners may prioritize financial returns over public welfare. Transparency in the bidding process, careful oversight, and strong regulatory frameworks are essential to ensure that private companies do not exploit public resources or engage in anti-competitive practices.

Moreover, while PPPs can provide financial relief for governments in the short term, they can create long-term obligations that may limit future policy flexibility. The government must ensure that the terms of the PPP are structured in such a way that it doesn't become financially burdensome over time. This includes monitoring the success of the project, ensuring that the private partner meets agreed-upon standards, and preventing excessive charges or tolls that could negatively impact the public.

In conclusion, Public-Private Partnerships present an innovative and practical solution for addressing the growing need for infrastructure development, particularly in an era of fiscal constraints. By combining public oversight with private sector efficiency and investment, PPPs can help governments deliver critical infrastructure projects on time, within budget, and with improved quality. However, for these partnerships to succeed, careful planning, transparent contracts, and rigorous oversight are required to mitigate risks and ensure that the public interest is protected. When executed well, PPPs can create a win-win scenario, enabling both public authorities and private companies to benefit from enhanced infrastructure, economic growth, and long-term sustainability.

Economic Impact of Modernizing Infrastructure

Modernizing infrastructure is one of the most effective strategies for stimulating economic growth, increasing productivity, and improving the overall quality of life. In an increasingly globalized and interconnected world, a nation's infrastructure—ranging from transportation systems and energy grids to communication networks and public utilities—forms the backbone of its economy. Well-functioning infrastructure enables businesses to operate more efficiently, reduces operating costs, and facilitates trade and commerce. Conversely, outdated or inefficient infrastructure can create bottlenecks, increase costs, and hinder economic growth. As countries invest in upgrading and modernizing their infrastructure, the long-term economic benefits can be substantial, impacting not only economic output but also social well-being and environmental sustainability.

One of the most immediate economic impacts of modernizing infrastructure is the creation of jobs. Infrastructure projects, such as building new roads, bridges, energy systems, and public transit networks, require a significant workforce, including engineers, construction workers, project managers, and specialized technicians. These projects often provide high-paying, skilled jobs in both the short and long term. For example, upgrading transportation networks can generate employment opportunities in construction, logistics, and supply chain management, while investments in energy infrastructure, such as renewable energy projects, create jobs in manufacturing, installation, and maintenance. Additionally, these job opportunities can provide a significant boost to local economies, especially in regions that may have faced economic stagnation due to limited investment in infrastructure.

Beyond job creation, modernizing infrastructure can lead to increased economic efficiency, which translates into higher productivity and reduced costs for businesses. For instance, improving transportation infrastructure, such as expanding highways, modernizing rail systems, and upgrading airports, facilitates the smoother movement of goods and services. Efficient transportation reduces supply chain delays, lowers shipping costs, and increases access to markets. In turn, businesses can operate more efficiently, which encourages investment, fosters innovation, and increases competitiveness on a global scale. In sectors like manufacturing and agriculture, where timely delivery of raw materials and finished products is essential, a well-maintained infrastructure can be a game-changer. The ability to efficiently move products from factories to markets opens up new opportunities for domestic and international trade.

Similarly, upgrading energy infrastructure, such as transitioning to smart grids, expanding renewable energy capacity, and modernizing power plants, can lead to substantial long-term economic benefits. A modern, reliable energy grid ensures a consistent supply of electricity, reduces energy costs, and improves the resilience of energy systems to extreme weather events or natural disasters. Renewable energy projects, in particular, can help reduce dependence on fossil fuels, mitigate climate change, and promote sustainable economic growth. Investing in clean energy infrastructure can also create green jobs in research, development, and energy production, while providing new growth opportunities in emerging industries. Furthermore, energy efficiency improvements can lower costs for businesses and households, making it easier for both sectors to thrive.

Another significant economic benefit of modernizing infrastructure is the improvement in the overall quality of life. Public infrastructure investments, such as the development of modern healthcare facilities, schools, and public transit, increase access to essential services, improve living conditions, and enhance the mobility of individuals. For example, public transportation systems that connect underserved communities to job centers can reduce transportation costs for low-income households, increase employment opportunities, and improve access to education and healthcare. When workers can easily commute to work, they spend less time in traffic, have more disposable income, and experience less stress, which can improve productivity across the economy.

Additionally, modernizing infrastructure can attract private investment. Businesses and investors are more likely to invest in areas with reliable infrastructure, which offers stability, predictability, and the promise of future returns. Cities and regions with modern transportation systems, efficient energy grids, and reliable internet networks are more likely to attract tech companies, manufacturers, and other industries seeking to operate in well-connected, forward-thinking environments. For example, Silicon Valley's growth was partly driven by its high-tech infrastructure, including fiber-optic internet and efficient transportation systems, which attracted tech giants such as Google, Apple, and Facebook. In turn, these investments lead to job creation, innovation, and long-term economic prosperity.

Modern infrastructure also plays a crucial role in fostering sustainability and reducing environmental impact. Transitioning to green infrastructure, such as renewable energy, electric vehicle charging networks, and energy-efficient buildings, can significantly reduce the carbon footprint of a country's economy. By investing in sustainable infrastructure, governments can meet climate goals, reduce reliance on fossil fuels, and contribute to global environmental efforts. Additionally, by creating eco-friendly infrastructure, businesses and consumers can lower operational costs, reduce waste, and create a more sustainable model for economic growth.

However, while the economic impact of modernizing infrastructure is clear, the challenges are significant. Infrastructure projects are costly and require substantial upfront investments, long-term planning, and coordination across various levels of government.

There are also political challenges in prioritizing and financing these projects, especially in times of budget constraints or fiscal austerity. Moreover, infrastructure projects often face delays and cost overruns, which can diminish their overall economic impact. To mitigate these challenges, it is essential to use innovative financing methods, such as public-private partnerships (PPPs), to bring in private sector capital and expertise.

In conclusion, modernizing infrastructure is a powerful tool for fostering economic prosperity. The immediate benefits include job creation, increased business efficiency, and improved quality of life, while the long-term impacts include enhanced competitiveness, energy sustainability, and environmental responsibility. As governments around the world face the pressures of population growth, urbanization, and climate change, investing in modern infrastructure will be critical to achieving sustainable economic growth and ensuring that future generations can enjoy the same—or even better—standards of living.

Chapter 7
The Role of Immigration in Economic Growth

Immigration has long been a driving force behind the economic success of many nations, particularly in the United States. Immigrants contribute to economic growth in a variety of ways, from enhancing the labor force to fostering innovation and entrepreneurship. Historically, immigrants have filled critical gaps in the labor market, contributed to the diversification of skills, and helped meet the demands of industries that rely on both low- and high-skilled workers. As the global economy becomes increasingly interconnected, the role of immigration in shaping national prosperity continues to evolve. For the U.S., immigration has been integral to maintaining its competitive edge in the global economy, particularly in sectors such as technology, healthcare, and manufacturing.

In addition to filling essential labor roles, immigrants bring new ideas, perspectives, and innovations that can drive economic dynamism. The United States, often described as a "nation of immigrants," has benefitted from the diverse cultural and intellectual contributions of its immigrant population. Immigrants are disproportionately represented in fields such as science, technology, engineering, and mathematics (STEM), where they drive research, development, and technological advancements. Many of the leading companies in Silicon Valley, for example, were founded or are led by immigrants, underscoring the important link between immigration and innovation. This chapter explores the multifaceted role that immigration plays in economic growth, analyzing both the direct and indirect contributions of immigrants to the economy.

While the economic benefits of immigration are clear, the debate over immigration policy remains contentious, particularly when it comes to issues such as border control, the allocation of resources, and the impact on domestic workers. Critics of immigration argue that an influx of immigrants can put pressure on public services, drive down wages for low-skilled workers, and contribute to unemployment in certain sectors. However, research has consistently shown that the overall economic impact of immigration is positive, as immigrants tend to complement rather than directly compete with native-born workers. By examining both the economic contributions and the challenges posed by immigration, this chapter will provide a comprehensive look at how immigration shapes the economic landscape, both in the U.S. and in other nations that rely on immigration as a source of growth.

Immigrant Labor and Its Contribution to Prosperity

Immigrant labor plays a vital role in the prosperity of many nations, particularly in economies that rely on diverse and dynamic workforces to fuel growth. In the United States, immigrants have historically been central to economic development, contributing significantly to industries ranging from agriculture and manufacturing to technology and healthcare. Immigrant labor helps fill crucial gaps in the labor market, providing both low-skilled workers for sectors requiring physical labor and highly skilled professionals in fields such as engineering, medicine, and technology. By understanding how immigrant labor drives prosperity, we can better appreciate the multifaceted contributions immigrants make to the economy, and the critical role they play in ensuring long-term economic growth.

One of the most obvious ways that immigrant labor contributes to prosperity is by addressing labor shortages in essential sectors. Immigrants often take on jobs that are difficult to fill with native-born workers, particularly in low-wage industries such as agriculture, construction, hospitality, and caregiving. These sectors are crucial to the functioning of the economy, as they provide basic services and goods that are in constant demand. Without immigrant workers, many of these industries would struggle to maintain productivity levels, leading to higher costs for businesses and consumers. For example, immigrant labor is essential in U.S. agriculture, where a significant portion of farm labor is provided by immigrants who pick crops, tend to livestock, and perform other essential tasks that support the nation's food production system. By filling these roles, immigrant workers help maintain the affordability and availability of goods, thereby contributing to economic stability and growth.

In addition to filling essential low-wage roles, immigrants also play an important part in the knowledge economy, especially in fields that require specialized skills and education. Immigrant labor is disproportionately represented in high-skilled industries, such as science, technology, engineering, and mathematics (STEM). Immigrants make up a significant portion of the workforce in tech companies, medical institutions, and research labs. Many immigrant professionals in the U.S. work as engineers, software developers, doctors, and researchers, driving innovation and technological advancement that can boost productivity, foster new industries, and improve living standards. Silicon Valley is a prime example of the economic contribution of immigrant labor, with many of its leading companies founded by immigrants or run by immigrant CEOs. These companies, including Apple, Google, and Tesla, have not only created jobs but have revolutionized industries globally. Immigrant labor in high-skill sectors fuels technological innovation, attracts foreign investment, and helps maintain the U.S.'s global leadership in various cutting-edge fields.

Moreover, immigrants contribute to economic prosperity through their entrepreneurial spirit. Immigrants are more likely to start their own businesses than native-born citizens, helping to stimulate local economies and create jobs. In fact, many of the most successful startups in the U.S. were founded by immigrants, spanning industries from technology to food service and retail. Immigrant entrepreneurs often bring fresh perspectives, ideas, and business practices that can lead to innovation and market growth. For instance, immigrant-owned small businesses account for a significant share of the U.S. economy, contributing billions of dollars in revenue and creating millions of jobs. These businesses not only create employment opportunities for other immigrants but also provide goods and services that contribute to the broader economy, from restaurants and convenience stores to tech startups and manufacturing enterprises.

In addition to their direct contributions, immigrants also play an essential role in the fiscal health of a nation. Contrary to some misconceptions, immigrants—particularly those who are working and paying taxes—contribute significantly to public finances. Immigrants pay income taxes, sales taxes, and social security contributions, which help fund essential public services such as education, healthcare, and infrastructure. Research consistently shows that immigrants contribute more in taxes than they receive in government services, particularly in the case of younger, working-age immigrants. Their contributions help support the elderly population and provide the revenue needed for vital social services. Furthermore, immigrants often bring new demand for services, products, and housing, which drives local economic growth and creates new opportunities for businesses in various sectors.

While immigrant labor provides undeniable benefits to the economy, there are also challenges to consider. Immigration policy, labor market dynamics, and the integration of immigrant workers into the broader workforce are complex issues that require careful management. Some critics argue that the influx of low-wage immigrant workers can put downward pressure on wages for native-born workers, particularly in certain industries. However, studies generally show that the economic benefits of immigration outweigh the drawbacks, as immigrant labor tends to complement rather than directly compete with native-born workers. Immigrants often take jobs that require different skill sets or work in industries that face labor shortages, thus filling gaps rather than displacing native workers.

In conclusion, immigrant labor is an integral component of economic prosperity, contributing to job creation, innovation, and fiscal health. Immigrants fill crucial roles in both low-skilled sectors, which support the day-to-day functioning of the economy, and high-skilled sectors, where they drive technological innovation and entrepreneurship. By addressing labor shortages, fostering innovation, and contributing to public finances, immigrants help sustain long-term economic growth and prosperity. As countries navigate the complexities of immigration, it is clear that immigrant labor will remain a driving force in ensuring a prosperous and dynamic future.

Trumponomics vs. Immigration Reform

The economic policies of Donald Trump, often referred to as Trumponomics, were marked by a strong emphasis on reducing taxes, deregulating industries, and prioritizing American workers through protectionist policies. At the same time, immigration reform was one of the most divisive and controversial areas of Trump's presidency, with his administration taking a hardline stance on immigration, seeking to limit both legal and illegal immigration into the U.S. The contrast between the economic objectives of Trumponomics and the approach to immigration reform highlights the tension between promoting economic growth and addressing the perceived challenges posed by immigration, particularly in the context of jobs and wages for native-born workers.

The Economic Philosophy of Trumponomics

Trumponomics was primarily focused on boosting American economic growth through supply-side economic policies. Central to Trump's vision was the belief that cutting taxes for businesses and individuals, reducing burdensome regulations, and encouraging American manufacturing would revitalize the U.S. economy. The Tax Cuts and Jobs Act of 2017 was a key element of this strategy, reducing the corporate tax rate from 35% to 21% and offering tax cuts for individuals, with the goal of stimulating investment and job creation. Trump's deregulatory efforts aimed to reduce the burden on businesses, particularly in industries such as energy, manufacturing, and financial services, arguing that fewer regulations would lead to more jobs and higher wages.

Additionally, Trump's trade policies, such as the renegotiation of NAFTA into the USMCA (United States-Mexico-Canada Agreement), were focused on addressing trade imbalances and protecting

American jobs, particularly in manufacturing. Trump's administration also sought to bring jobs back to the U.S. through tariffs on foreign imports, particularly from China, arguing that American workers were losing out to unfair competition from countries with lower labor standards and lower wages.

While these policies were geared toward boosting domestic job growth and revitalizing American manufacturing, they also contributed to a perception that immigration was a threat to American jobs, particularly in lower-wage sectors. The rise in anti-immigrant sentiment was reflected in Trump's tough stance on immigration reform, which included building a wall along the U.S.-Mexico border, limiting refugee admissions, and cracking down on illegal immigration.

The Immigration Reform Agenda

Trump's approach to immigration reform was built on a combination of enforcement measures and restrictive immigration policies. His administration focused on reducing illegal immigration, often framing it as a threat to national security and the American labor market. The border wall, which became one of Trump's most prominent promises, was designed to prevent illegal immigration, particularly from Central American countries. Additionally, the Trump administration sought to limit legal immigration by reducing the number of refugees and asylum seekers allowed into the country, as well as restricting the issuance of certain visas, including those for high-skilled workers under the H-1B visa program.

One of the most contentious aspects of Trump's immigration policy was its emphasis on reducing the number of low-wage immigrant workers entering the U.S. In particular, Trump's administration focused on limiting immigration from countries in

Latin America and the Middle East, which it argued were contributing to job displacement and wage suppression for native-born Americans. This perspective was rooted in the belief that reducing immigration would allow more job opportunities for U.S. workers, especially in industries like construction, hospitality, and agriculture, where many immigrants, both legal and undocumented, are employed.

However, critics of Trump's immigration policies argued that this approach was counterproductive to the goals of Trumponomics. Immigrants, they contended, were not just filling low-wage jobs but were also contributing to the U.S. economy in significant ways. Immigrants make up a large proportion of workers in critical sectors, such as healthcare, technology, and agriculture, and their skills, labor, and entrepreneurial spirit have been integral to the country's economic dynamism. In industries like technology, for example, immigrants play a crucial role in driving innovation and contributing to the growth of high-tech companies. Additionally, immigrant entrepreneurs have founded many successful businesses, contributing to job creation and economic development.

The Tension Between Trumponomics and Immigration Reform

The tension between *Trumponomics* and immigration reform stems from the conflicting views on the role of immigration in economic growth. On one hand, *Trumponomics* seeks to protect American workers by reducing competition from foreign workers, particularly in low-skilled sectors, through restrictive immigration policies. On the other hand, the evidence shows that immigration has long been a driver of economic prosperity in the U.S., helping to fill labor gaps, contribute to innovation, and sustain industries that rely on both low- and high-skilled labor.

While Trump's immigration policies were aimed at protecting native-born workers and promoting American industries, critics argued that limiting immigration could hinder economic growth in the long term. Immigrants, particularly those with high levels of education and specialized skills, contribute to technological advancement and help to drive productivity growth in key sectors of the economy. Furthermore, immigrants contribute to the economy by paying taxes, purchasing goods and services, and creating demand for housing, healthcare, and education.

Moreover, the long-term economic growth associated with Trumponomics depended on a highly skilled and adaptable workforce, which immigration could help provide. Limiting immigration from countries with large pools of skilled labor, such as India and China, could lead to talent shortages in technology, engineering, and other high-growth industries.

In conclusion, while *Trumponomics* focused on revitalizing American industries through tax cuts, deregulation, and protectionist trade policies, the approach to immigration reform often stood in contrast to these economic goals. While reducing immigration may have seemed beneficial to some sectors, it posed risks to overall economic growth by limiting the labor force and reducing the flow of skilled workers and entrepreneurs. For the U.S. to continue thriving economically, policymakers need to find a way to balance the benefits of controlling immigration with the undeniable contributions immigrants make to the economy. Achieving this balance would allow the U.S. to maintain its competitive edge while ensuring that American workers, both native-born and immigrant, can thrive in an evolving global economy.

The Economic Debate: Protectionism or Inclusivity?

The debate between protectionism and inclusivity lies at the heart of many contemporary economic discussions, especially in the context of global trade, immigration, and economic growth. Protectionism advocates for policies that shield domestic industries from foreign competition, often through tariffs, quotas, and other trade barriers, with the aim of preserving jobs, fostering local businesses, and maintaining national security. Inclusivity, on the other hand, emphasizes the integration of global markets, advocating for free trade, open borders, and collaboration among nations to drive collective prosperity. Both approaches offer distinct benefits and challenges, and the choice between them often depends on economic priorities, political ideologies, and the specific circumstances of a nation.

Protectionism: Safeguarding Domestic Interests

Protectionism is often seen as a way to shield domestic industries from foreign competition, particularly when those industries face challenges from cheaper or more efficient products imported from other countries. The argument for protectionism is particularly strong in sectors where countries face trade imbalances or where domestic industries are struggling to compete with low-cost producers. For instance, many policymakers in the U.S. and Europe have argued that tariffs on foreign goods, particularly from China and other developing nations, are necessary to protect jobs in manufacturing and prevent the erosion of local industries.

One of the key benefits of protectionism is that it can support the growth of domestic industries, especially in developing or transitioning economies. By limiting foreign competition, protectionist policies can create a more stable environment for local businesses to thrive, invest in innovation, and expand production. This can be especially important in sectors critical to national security, such as energy, agriculture, and defense. Protectionism can also help protect workers from wage suppression due to an influx of cheap foreign labor, which some argue leads to job losses and economic inequality in certain sectors.

Furthermore, protectionism is often promoted as a means of preserving cultural and economic sovereignty. By prioritizing local industries, countries can reduce their dependence on global supply chains, which are increasingly vulnerable to disruptions from geopolitical tensions, natural disasters, or global pandemics. In the face of such uncertainties, protectionist measures can be seen as a way to create a more resilient and self-sufficient economy, one that is less exposed to the risks of an interconnected world.

However, the downsides of protectionism are significant. While it can protect certain industries in the short term, long-term protectionism can lead to inefficiencies, reduced innovation, and higher costs for consumers. Industries that are shielded from competition may have less incentive to innovate, resulting in stagnation and reduced productivity. Protectionism also raises the risk of trade wars, where countries retaliate with tariffs and other barriers, leading to reduced global trade and economic uncertainty. Additionally, consumers often face higher prices for goods that are produced domestically, which can disproportionately affect lower-income households.

Inclusivity: Embracing Globalization for Growth

In contrast to protectionism, inclusivity is based on the belief that global cooperation and the free flow of goods, services, and labor lead to greater economic prosperity. Proponents of inclusivity argue that by embracing free trade, countries can access cheaper goods, lower production costs, and more diverse markets for their products. The benefits of inclusivity are often associated with the theory of comparative advantage, which posits that countries should specialize in the production of goods and services in which they are most efficient and trade them with other nations. This leads to a more efficient global economy and allows consumers to access a wider variety of goods at lower prices.

Inclusivity also highlights the importance of immigration and the movement of people, asserting that diverse labor forces lead to greater innovation and economic dynamism. Immigrants often fill essential gaps in the labor market, particularly in industries like technology, healthcare, and agriculture, where demand for skilled and unskilled workers often exceeds domestic supply. In this sense, inclusivity encourages a globalized economy where talent, ideas, and resources flow freely across borders, creating opportunities for individuals, businesses, and nations alike.

One of the key advantages of inclusivity is the potential for long-term growth. By integrating economies and markets, countries can tap into new opportunities for trade, investment, and technological exchange. Global supply chains allow companies to access raw materials, labor, and expertise from around the world, enabling them to produce goods more efficiently and at lower costs. This often results in higher economic growth rates, increased living standards, and the creation of new jobs in sectors such as finance, technology, and services.

Moreover, inclusivity fosters greater cooperation between countries, leading to peace and stability. By engaging in international trade agreements, such as the World Trade Organization (WTO) or regional pacts like the European Union (EU), countries can create frameworks for resolving disputes, harmonizing standards, and promoting mutual benefits. This interconnectedness can help prevent conflicts and foster diplomatic relationships, as countries become more dependent on one another for economic success.

However, the inclusivity model also has its challenges. While it promotes economic growth, the benefits are not always equally distributed. Some industries, especially those in sectors vulnerable to global competition, may suffer as a result of trade liberalization. Workers in low-wage jobs may experience job displacement as companies move production to countries with lower labor costs. This can exacerbate income inequality and lead to social unrest, as communities feel left behind by the global economy. Furthermore, global supply chains can sometimes lead to environmental degradation and exploitation of workers in developing nations, which raises ethical concerns about the costs of free trade.

Balancing the Two Approaches

The debate between protectionism and inclusivity is not a binary one; rather, it requires a nuanced approach. The ideal economic model likely involves a balance between the two, where countries protect certain industries for national security or public welfare reasons while also embracing the benefits of global trade and cooperation. Policies should be designed to mitigate the negative impacts of both approaches—providing support and retraining for workers displaced by globalization while fostering innovation and competition in protected sectors. By creating policies that allow for both local economic protection and global economic integration, nations can benefit from the best of both worlds—sustaining growth, promoting fairness, and ensuring long-term prosperity.

In conclusion, the choice between protectionism and inclusivity is not just an economic debate but a reflection of a nation's priorities and values. Protectionism offers short-term gains in certain sectors but risks long-term inefficiency and global isolation, while inclusivity offers the potential for sustained growth and innovation but requires careful management of its social and economic consequences. Finding a balance that maximizes the benefits of both approaches is key to ensuring a stable, prosperous future in an increasingly interconnected world.

Chapter 8
The Impact on Global Markets and Geopolitics

The interaction between economic policies, global markets, and geopolitics has become more complex and interconnected in recent decades, influencing everything from trade relationships to international diplomacy. As nations strive to protect their economic interests, the implications of economic policies ripple across borders, affecting markets, industries, and international alliances. In the context of *Trumponomics*, which has heavily emphasized protectionism, tariffs, and reshaping global trade agreements, the global economy has witnessed profound shifts. These policies have not only impacted the U.S. economy but have also had far-reaching consequences for markets and countries worldwide, reshaping the dynamics of international trade and diplomatic relations.

At the core of the discussion on the impact of *Trumponomics* on global markets is the rise of protectionist measures, such as tariffs and trade barriers. The U.S.'s withdrawal from international trade agreements like the Trans-Pacific Partnership (TPP) and its renegotiation of NAFTA into the USMCA (United States-Mexico-Canada Agreement) marked a shift towards more isolationist and nationalistic trade policies. These actions have reverberated through global markets, creating uncertainty and volatility, particularly in sectors reliant on free trade, such as manufacturing, technology, and agriculture. Tariffs imposed on countries like China have led to retaliatory measures, further disrupting supply chains and global trade flows. The broader impact of these shifts on global economic stability, market access, and the rules of international trade is a critical area of exploration in this chapter.

The changing dynamics of global geopolitics also play a significant role in shaping the impact of economic policies on global markets. As *Trumponomics* prioritizes American economic interests, there has been a noticeable shift in the U.S.'s approach to international partnerships and alliances. The emphasis on "America First" has strained traditional alliances with Europe and some Asian partners, while simultaneously challenging long-standing global institutions like the World Trade Organization (WTO). These geopolitical shifts, compounded by rising nationalism in other parts of the world, have led to a new era of economic and political competition, where countries are increasingly turning inward and reevaluating their positions on the global stage. This chapter will delve into how these changes have reshaped global markets, influenced diplomatic relationships, and shifted the balance of power in international politics.

US-China Trade Relations and the Global Economy

The trade relationship between the United States and China has long been one of the most significant drivers of global economic dynamics. As the world's two largest economies, the economic policies and trade practices of both countries have profound implications for global markets, international trade agreements, and geopolitical relations. Over the past few decades, China's rise as an economic powerhouse has shifted the global balance of power, creating a complex and often contentious trade relationship with the

U.S. The trade tension between the U.S. and China reached a new peak under President Donald Trump's administration, which introduced a series of protectionist measures aimed at addressing perceived trade imbalances, unfair practices, and intellectual property theft. These actions not only impacted the U.S. and China but also had far-reaching consequences for the global economy.

One of the central issues in U.S.-China trade relations is the significant trade deficit that the U.S. runs with China. The U.S. imports far more from China than it exports, which has been a longstanding point of contention. According to the U.S. Census Bureau, the trade deficit with China reached nearly $400 billion annually in the years leading up to the Trump administration, prompting concerns about the loss of manufacturing jobs and the erosion of the U.S. industrial base. Under Trump, the U.S. sought to reduce this deficit by imposing tariffs on a wide range of Chinese goods, including steel, aluminum, electronics, and consumer products. The goal was to make Chinese products more expensive and less competitive in the U.S. market, thereby encouraging American consumers to purchase domestic goods and reducing the trade imbalance.

In response, China retaliated with its own tariffs on American products, particularly agricultural goods such as soybeans, pork, and wheat. This tit-for-tat tariff war not only disrupted the supply chains between the two countries but also created uncertainty in global markets, especially in industries that rely heavily on trade with both the U.S. and China. For example, the tech sector, which is deeply integrated with Chinese manufacturing, faced price hikes and supply chain disruptions as tariffs affected the flow of components and finished goods. Similarly, farmers in the U.S. were hurt by China's tariffs on agricultural exports, leading to a decline in sales to the

Chinese market, which was a major consumer of U.S. agricultural products. The ripple effects of these trade tensions extended beyond the U.S. and China, impacting global supply chains, commodity prices, and international trade agreements.

The trade war between the U.S. and China also raised concerns about the long-term consequences for the global economy. As two of the world's largest economies, U.S.-China trade relations play a crucial role in maintaining global economic stability. The imposition of tariffs and trade barriers disrupted not only bilateral trade but also global supply chains, leading to increased costs for businesses worldwide. Multinational companies that rely on Chinese manufacturing and assembly lines, as well as those that depend on the U.S. market for their products, were forced to navigate higher costs and changing trade dynamics. In industries like electronics, automobiles, and pharmaceuticals, companies that source materials and components from China found themselves facing higher production costs and delays in delivery. This uncertainty made it harder for businesses to plan for the future, leading to reduced investment and slower growth in the global economy.

Beyond tariffs, other aspects of the trade relationship between the U.S. and China have also shaped global economic dynamics. One key issue is intellectual property rights, with the U.S. accusing China of engaging in unfair practices such as forced technology transfers and cyber-espionage. The U.S. government argued that China's policies were designed to steal intellectual property from American companies and force them to hand over their most valuable technologies in exchange for market access. This issue was central to the trade negotiations between the U.S. and China, with the Trump administration pushing for stronger protections for American intellectual property in any trade agreement. The U.S. also sought to address China's industrial policies, which were seen as unfairly subsidizing Chinese companies and giving them an advantage in the global market. These concerns were not only about the direct impact on U.S. businesses but also about the broader implications for the global economic order, as China's rise in key industries like technology and telecommunications was viewed as a challenge to U.S. dominance.

The trade war between the U.S. and China also had geopolitical implications, as it influenced the broader balance of power in international relations. China, seeking to expand its influence in the global economy, made strategic investments in infrastructure projects through initiatives like the Belt and Road Initiative (BRI), which aimed to strengthen China's economic ties with countries across Asia, Africa, and Europe. These efforts were seen as a way for China to assert its influence and challenge U.S. dominance in global trade. The U.S., in turn, responded by seeking to counter China's rise through tariffs, sanctions, and efforts to isolate China in international institutions like the World Trade Organization (WTO).

In conclusion, the trade relations between the U.S. and China are a cornerstone of global economic stability and prosperity. The protectionist measures introduced under *Trumponomics*, including tariffs and trade barriers, reshaped the dynamics of U.S.-China trade and had far-reaching consequences for global markets. While these policies were aimed at reducing the U.S. trade deficit and addressing issues such as intellectual property theft, they also created significant disruptions in global supply chains and raised concerns about the long-term impact on the global economy. As both nations continue to navigate their trade relationship, the U.S.-China trade conflict will remain a key factor in shaping global economic and geopolitical dynamics in the 21st century.

America's Influence on Emerging Markets

The United States has long been one of the most influential players in the global economy, and its economic policies, financial markets, and corporate interests have a significant impact on emerging markets around the world. Emerging markets—economies that are in the process of rapid growth and industrialization—are particularly sensitive to developments in the U.S. due to their increasing integration into the global financial system. America's influence on these markets can be seen in various aspects, from trade relationships and capital flows to geopolitical strategies and the impact of U.S. monetary policy. While American influence has contributed to the growth of emerging markets, it has also created challenges, particularly in terms of economic vulnerability and dependency.

Trade and Investment

One of the most direct ways that the U.S. influences emerging markets is through trade and investment. As the world's largest economy, the U.S. is a key trading partner for many emerging market countries, particularly those in Latin America, Asia, and Africa. American companies invest heavily in emerging markets, seeking access to new consumer markets, cheaper labor, and raw materials. For example, U.S. multinational corporations have been active in sectors such as manufacturing, technology, natural resources, and agriculture in countries like China, India, Brazil, and South Africa. These investments not only contribute to the growth of these economies but also provide critical infrastructure, technology, and expertise that help local markets develop and modernize.

The U.S. is also a major source of foreign direct investment (FDI) in emerging markets, and this capital flow helps stimulate economic growth by providing the necessary funds for businesses to expand and develop. American investments in emerging markets often lead to the creation of jobs, improvements in local industries, and increased tax revenues for governments. Additionally, American trade policies—such as preferential trade agreements, such as the U.S.-Mexico-Canada Agreement (USMCA), or through the Generalized System of Preferences (GSP)—can offer developing countries access to the American market, stimulating their exports and providing further opportunities for growth.

Financial Markets and Capital Flows

Another crucial aspect of America's influence on emerging markets is the role of the U.S. financial system and capital markets. The U.S. dollar is the world's primary reserve currency, and most international trade, particularly in commodities like oil and gold, is conducted in U.S. dollars. This gives the U.S. significant leverage over global financial transactions and impacts emerging markets in profound ways. For example, fluctuations in the value of the U.S. dollar can affect the debt burdens of emerging market countries, particularly those with significant dollar-denominated debt. A stronger dollar can make it more expensive for these countries to repay their debts, potentially leading to financial instability.

Moreover, U.S. interest rates, set by the Federal Reserve, influence capital flows into emerging markets. When the Federal Reserve raises interest rates, it can lead to capital outflows from emerging markets as investors seek higher returns in the U.S. This can result in currency depreciation, increased inflation, and higher borrowing costs for developing economies. Conversely, when the Federal Reserve cuts rates, it can lead to increased capital inflows into emerging markets, boosting their economic growth but also increasing the risk of asset bubbles. Emerging market economies are thus highly sensitive to U.S. monetary policy, which has implications for their financial stability and long-term growth prospects.

Geopolitical Influence and Economic Diplomacy

America's geopolitical influence is another way it impacts emerging markets. Through foreign aid, economic diplomacy, and international institutions such as the World Bank and the International Monetary Fund (IMF), the U.S. has significant sway over the economic policies and development strategies of emerging economies. U.S. foreign aid is often tied to political and economic reforms, and the country has used its position to promote free-market capitalism, democratic governance, and the rule of law in many developing nations. This influence has helped integrate emerging markets into the global trading system, providing them with access to global markets, technology, and investment.

However, America's influence in geopolitics can also create challenges for emerging markets, particularly when U.S. foreign policy interests conflict with the priorities of these nations. For example, trade sanctions and economic embargoes, such as those imposed on countries like Iran and Venezuela, can severely disrupt economic growth in these markets. Additionally, the U.S.'s influence in global institutions has at times been criticized for pushing policies that favor American economic interests, sometimes at the expense of the development goals of emerging markets. As a result, some countries may seek to diversify their economic relationships by engaging more with emerging powers like China or Russia, reducing their dependence on the U.S. and its economic policies.

Challenges and Opportunities

While America's influence has undoubtedly contributed to the growth and development of emerging markets, it has also exposed them to certain risks. The global dominance of the U.S. dollar, the interdependence of financial markets, and U.S.-led economic institutions create vulnerabilities for emerging economies, particularly in times of global economic uncertainty or U.S. policy shifts. Emerging markets that rely heavily on exports to the U.S. or are indebted in dollars can experience financial strain when U.S. policies change, making them more susceptible to external shocks.

However, the economic relationship between the U.S. and emerging markets also presents significant opportunities for growth. As developing nations continue to industrialize and urbanize, they represent important markets for U.S. goods and services. The growing middle class in countries like India and China offers vast opportunities for American companies to expand their consumer base. Additionally, as global trade expands, emerging markets are increasingly involved in international supply chains, with American companies at the center of technological and industrial innovation.

America's influence on emerging markets is a complex and multifaceted relationship that shapes the economic trajectory of developing nations. Through trade, investment, financial markets, and geopolitical power, the U.S. plays a crucial role in facilitating the growth of emerging economies while also creating challenges and dependencies. As these markets continue to grow, America's economic policies will remain a central factor in shaping their development, both in terms of opportunities and vulnerabilities. The future of global economic relations will depend on how emerging markets balance their reliance on the U.S. with efforts to diversify their economic relationships and ensure long-term, sustainable growth.

Trumponomics and Global Stability

Trumponomics refers to the economic policies enacted during Donald Trump's presidency, marked by a distinctive combination of protectionism, tax cuts, deregulation, and a focus on "America First." These policies were designed to boost the U.S. economy by stimulating domestic growth, reducing the trade deficit, and encouraging American businesses to invest and manufacture within the country. While *Trumponomics* has had notable effects on the U.S. economy, its impact on global stability has been more complicated. The ripple effects of Trump's economic agenda have shaped global trade, financial markets, and diplomatic relations, creating both opportunities and challenges for economies around the world.

Trade Protectionism and Its Global Consequences

One of the most defining aspects of *Trumponomics* was its embrace of protectionist trade policies. Trump's administration aimed to reduce the U.S. trade deficit by imposing tariffs on goods from countries with whom the U.S. had significant trade imbalances, most notably China. The introduction of tariffs on steel, aluminum, and a wide range of Chinese goods sparked a trade war that reverberated through the global economy. These tariffs led to retaliatory measures from other countries, which created uncertainty and instability in global markets. Countries reliant on trade with the U.S. faced disruptions in their exports, leading to economic slowdowns in some regions.

While the goal of these protectionist policies was to protect American industries and jobs, particularly in manufacturing and agriculture, the broader global economy felt the strain. Global supply chains were disrupted, and multinational companies that depended on seamless trade between countries faced increased costs and uncertainty. For emerging markets, this was especially challenging as trade wars threatened their access to key markets, and the U.S.'s reduced global engagement made it more difficult to secure investment. For example, China's retaliatory tariffs affected American farmers, particularly in rural areas, leading to decreased agricultural exports, while at the same time reducing China's ability to access U.S. markets for products ranging from technology to automobiles.

Financial Market Volatility

Trumponomics also had a profound impact on global financial markets. The uncertainty created by trade tensions, coupled with Trump's unpredictable rhetoric and policies, led to market volatility. While U.S. stock markets initially surged due to corporate tax cuts and deregulation in key sectors, particularly energy and finance, global markets experienced periods of instability. The risk of trade wars, combined with Trump's unpredictable stance on global issues, led investors to hedge their bets, particularly in markets in Asia and Europe. The U.S. dollar, often seen as a safe haven, experienced fluctuations as a result of changing U.S. monetary policy and tariffs, which had direct consequences for international trade and investment.

Additionally, Trump's administration's stance on international economic agreements, such as withdrawing from the Trans-Pacific Partnership (TPP) and renegotiating the North American Free Trade Agreement (NAFTA) into the United States-Mexico-Canada Agreement (USMCA), raised questions about the future of global economic governance. By pulling back from multilateral trade agreements and seeking to rewrite deals on a bilateral basis, Trump's policies signaled a shift towards economic nationalism, undermining the role of international institutions like the World Trade

Organization (WTO) and reducing the predictability that these bodies provide to global markets.

Geopolitical Instability and Diplomacy

Beyond economics, *Trumponomics* has had broader implications for global stability, particularly in the realm of geopolitics. Trump's "America First" foreign policy, while focused on bolstering U.S. interests, often led to strained relationships with key allies. His withdrawal from the Paris Climate Agreement, the Iran nuclear deal, and the Transatlantic Trade and Investment Partnership (TTIP) with the European Union reflected a willingness to act unilaterally, which unsettled international relations and global governance structures. His approach to global diplomacy, including trade negotiations with China, created a zero-sum mentality that made it more difficult for countries to cooperate on international issues such as climate change, security, and migration.

Trump's policies also contributed to the rise of nationalism and populism in other parts of the world. Leaders in Europe and Asia, seeing Trump's stance as a model for advancing national interests, began embracing protectionist and isolationist policies of their own. This led to a fracturing of the previously strong international cooperation on economic and geopolitical issues, increasing instability in regions that had been central to global peace and security. Trump's approach to alliances, such as his frequent criticism of NATO, further strained relationships with traditional allies, leaving the U.S. less engaged in cooperative efforts that had long been a cornerstone of global stability.

Long-Term Impact on Global Stability

The long-term implications of *Trumponomics* on global stability are still unfolding. The policies of the Trump administration have contributed to a more fragmented global economic system, where economic nationalism, protectionism, and trade wars have taken center stage. While some argue that these policies have led to stronger economic growth and job creation in the U.S., particularly in manufacturing, the global consequences have been more mixed. Emerging markets, global supply chains, and multinational corporations have faced increased risks and costs, while geopolitical tensions have risen due to America's more isolationist approach.

Furthermore, the global balance of power is being reshaped as countries like China and the European Union, which have been increasingly at odds with U.S. policies, seek to assert their influence in global economic governance. China, for example, has continued its expansionist economic policies through initiatives like the Belt and Road Initiative (BRI), presenting an alternative to the U.S.-dominated global economic order. As the U.S. pulls back from multilateralism, other nations are stepping up to fill the void, creating a multipolar world in which economic and geopolitical stability is more uncertain than it has been in decades.

In conclusion, *Trumponomics* has played a key role in shaping the current state of global economic and geopolitical stability. While the policies enacted under Trump have contributed to some domestic economic successes, they have also led to increased volatility, uncertainty, and tensions in the global arena. The shift towards protectionism, combined with a more isolationist stance on diplomacy, has created a fragmented world order, raising questions about the future of international cooperation, global trade, and long-term stability.

Chapter 9
Managing Debt and Fiscal Responsibility

Managing national debt and ensuring fiscal responsibility are fundamental to maintaining economic stability and long-term prosperity. For many countries, including the United States, government debt has risen to historically high levels, driven by a combination of spending on social programs, defense, and economic stimulus measures. Under the Trump administration, the debate over managing debt became more prominent, particularly with the introduction of large tax cuts and increased spending on defense. While these policies were aimed at stimulating economic growth, they also contributed to a rise in the federal deficit and national debt, sparking ongoing discussions about the long-term sustainability of such fiscal policies. This chapter will explore the challenges and implications of managing national debt, focusing on the trade-offs between stimulating short-term growth and ensuring long-term fiscal health.

Fiscal responsibility, traditionally viewed as the responsibility of governments to balance budgets and avoid excessive borrowing, is a critical issue in discussions about national debt. Advocates for fiscal discipline argue that runaway government debt can lead to higher interest rates, reduced investment in public infrastructure, and an increased burden on future generations. On the other hand, critics of austerity measures assert that strategic borrowing can support economic growth, particularly during times of economic crisis or when investing in infrastructure, education, and other long-term priorities. The Trump administration's fiscal policies, which included tax cuts and significant increases in military spending, often leaned towards stimulating immediate growth rather than prioritizing debt reduction. As a result, the U.S. witnessed a sharp increase in its national debt during his time in office, raising concerns about the future trajectory of government finances.

This chapter will also examine the broader global implications of national debt management. Countries with high levels of debt face potential challenges in maintaining investor confidence and securing affordable financing, especially in times of economic uncertainty. As the U.S. economy remains heavily interconnected with global markets, its fiscal health is of particular concern to international investors and trading partners. The economic policies of one nation can have ripple effects across the global financial system, influencing exchange rates, trade balances, and capital flows. Through this exploration, we will address the delicate balance between fiscal responsibility and economic growth, the risks of excessive debt accumulation, and the potential solutions to ensure sustainable public finances in the future.

The National Debt: Is Trumponomics Sustainable?

The national debt of the United States has been a source of concern for decades, but during the Trump administration, the conversation surrounding the sustainability of U.S. fiscal policy reached new heights. *Trumponomics*—which emphasized tax cuts, deregulation, and an "America First" approach—was designed to stimulate economic growth by fostering a more competitive business environment. However, the policies that fueled this growth, particularly the 2017 Tax Cuts and Jobs Act (TCJA) and increased military and infrastructure spending, also significantly expanded the national debt. This chapter examines whether the *Trumponomics* approach to fiscal policy is sustainable in the long term, considering the implications of rising debt and the potential impact on the U.S. economy and global markets.

Tax Cuts and the Growing Deficit

One of the core tenets of *Trumponomics* was the promise of lower taxes for individuals and corporations. The TCJA of 2017 slashed the corporate tax rate from 35% to 21% and provided temporary tax cuts for individuals. While these measures were aimed at stimulating investment, encouraging corporate repatriation of foreign earnings, and increasing disposable income for consumers, they also had significant fiscal consequences. The tax cuts reduced government revenue by an estimated $1.5 trillion over a decade, exacerbating the federal deficit, which had already been rising due to increased spending in other areas, such as defense and entitlement programs.

Critics of the tax cuts argued that while the reduction in corporate tax rates was designed to stimulate economic growth, it also contributed to an unsustainable rise in the national debt. The U.S. federal deficit rose significantly following the implementation of the tax cuts, from $665 billion in 2017 to over $1 trillion by 2020. Despite claims that tax cuts would pay for themselves through higher economic growth, the immediate effects were mixed. While the economy did see a short-term boost, particularly in corporate profits and the stock market, the promised sustained long-term growth did not materialize as anticipated. Instead, the U.S. continued to see budget deficits soar, which contributed to a substantial increase in the national debt.

Increased Spending: Defense and Domestic Programs

In addition to tax cuts, the Trump administration also oversaw a significant increase in government spending. While the administration pushed for a reduction in federal bureaucracy and public spending in some areas, military spending saw substantial growth. Trump pushed for a $700 billion defense budget in 2018, which was part of a broader military spending spree aimed at strengthening the U.S. military presence around the world. This increase in defense spending, along with additional spending on infrastructure and domestic programs, further contributed to the rise in the national debt. While these investments were intended to stimulate job creation and strengthen the U.S.'s position globally, they also added billions of dollars to the deficit.

Moreover, the COVID-19 pandemic exacerbated the already rising debt. In response to the economic collapse triggered by the pandemic, the U.S. government passed several stimulus packages, including the $2.2 trillion Coronavirus Aid, Relief, and Economic Security (CARES) Act in March 2020. These measures were necessary to support American businesses, individuals, and healthcare systems, but they also led to a sharp increase in government borrowing. By the time Trump left office in January 2021, the national debt had surpassed $27 trillion, a figure that is projected to continue rising as the pandemic response efforts unfold and recovery measures continue.

The Sustainability of Trumponomics

The sustainability of *Trumponomics* and its approach to fiscal policy hinges on the ability to manage rising national debt without causing long-term harm to the U.S. economy. Debt in and of itself is not inherently harmful; many countries with high debt levels maintain strong economies. However, when debt levels rise too quickly or become unsustainable, the risks increase. For the U.S., much of its debt is financed through the issuance of Treasury bonds, which are seen as one of the safest investments globally. This has allowed the U.S. to borrow at relatively low interest rates. However, if investor confidence in U.S. fiscal policy wanes or if interest rates rise significantly, the cost of servicing this debt could increase, placing pressure on future budgets and potentially crowding out other important government spending.

In the long term, the U.S. faces two key challenges: first, maintaining investor confidence in its ability to manage its debt, and second, ensuring that the growth generated by tax cuts and increased spending is sufficient to offset the rising debt. If economic growth fails to meet expectations, and the government continues to rely on borrowing to fund its deficits, the debt could become unsustainable. This scenario could lead to higher inflation, increased borrowing costs, and potentially a loss of confidence in the U.S. dollar.

Additionally, *Trumponomics*' reliance on debt-fueled stimulus raises concerns about intergenerational equity. While the policies may provide short-term economic benefits, the growing national debt will likely place a burden on future generations. As the U.S. government borrows to fund current policies, future taxpayers will be responsible for repaying the debt and managing the economic fallout from increased borrowing. The challenge for policymakers is finding a way to balance short-term economic stimulus with long-term fiscal sustainability.

The sustainability of *Trumponomics* and its reliance on tax cuts and increased spending will depend on the ability to balance fiscal policy with economic growth. While the tax cuts and spending increases did provide short-term boosts to the economy, they have also led to a significant rise in the national debt. The ability of the U.S. government to manage this debt without triggering inflation, higher interest rates, or reduced confidence in U.S. Treasury bonds will be crucial to maintaining long-term economic stability. As the U.S. faces ongoing challenges, such as the COVID-19 recovery and potential global economic instability, the future of *Trumponomics* will ultimately depend on whether the benefits of fiscal stimulus can be sustained without exacerbating the nation's fiscal challenges. The U.S. will need to make difficult choices regarding tax policy, spending, and debt management to ensure that the economic growth achieved during the Trump years does not come at the expense of future generations.

Budget Cuts vs. Investment in Growth

The debate between budget cuts and investment in growth is one of the most critical issues in economic policy, as it directly influences the direction of a nation's fiscal future. On one hand, proponents of budget cuts argue that reducing government spending is necessary to control the national debt, improve fiscal discipline, and ensure long-term financial stability. They believe that by trimming unnecessary expenses and reducing the size of government, the economy can grow more sustainably, allowing for tax cuts and less public borrowing. On the other hand, advocates of investment in growth argue that strategic spending, particularly in infrastructure, education, and technology, is essential for driving economic prosperity in the long run. They argue that cutting investments in growth can lead to stagnation, reduced competitiveness, and missed opportunities in a rapidly changing global economy.

Budget cuts typically come into play when governments face growing deficits or national debt. Fiscal conservatives and some economists argue that excessive government spending crowds out private sector activity, leading to inefficient allocation of resources and slowing down the economy. In their view, reducing public sector expenditures forces governments to make more prudent choices, ensuring that funds are spent where they are most needed. By cutting costs in areas such as social programs, defense, and public services, governments can reduce their borrowing needs and create a more balanced budget. This approach, they argue, will ensure that future generations are not burdened by high debt levels and that the country maintains fiscal health. Moreover, by lowering taxes, especially for businesses, the private sector is encouraged to invest, grow, and create jobs, thus boosting the economy through market-driven forces.

However, the emphasis on budget cuts often overlooks the long-term benefits of investment in critical sectors. In reality, investment in infrastructure, education, and technology can provide substantial returns by fostering economic growth, creating jobs, and improving the efficiency of the economy. For instance, building and upgrading transportation networks, energy grids, and digital infrastructure can help reduce costs for businesses, facilitate trade, and increase productivity. These investments, while expensive in the short term, can help create a more competitive environment for businesses, leading to higher wages and a more dynamic economy. Similarly, investing in education and workforce development prepares future generations for the challenges of an increasingly globalized and technology-driven world. Without these investments, countries risk falling behind as they are unable to harness the full potential of their labor force.

Furthermore, investment in growth through government spending can help smooth out the volatility of the business cycle. During economic downturns, when private sector spending falters, government investments in infrastructure, social services, and other areas can act as a stabilizing force, creating jobs and providing a cushion against the effects of recession. By maintaining a steady flow of investment, governments can help sustain consumer confidence and ensure that the economy does not fall into a prolonged slump. In contrast, aggressive budget cuts during times of economic hardship can exacerbate recessions, as they reduce demand, increase unemployment, and lead to reduced public services. This can create a cycle of economic contraction that becomes difficult to reverse.

Ultimately, the challenge lies in finding the right balance between budget cuts and investment in growth. While it is essential to maintain fiscal discipline and ensure that government debt remains manageable, cutting back too aggressively on investment can harm long-term prosperity. Governments must prioritize investments that offer high returns in terms of future economic growth and competitiveness, such as in education, infrastructure, and technology. These investments not only stimulate job creation and innovation but also lay the foundation for sustained economic success. At the same time, efforts to reduce wasteful spending and improve the efficiency of government programs are necessary to prevent the bloating of public debt.

In conclusion, the debate between budget cuts and investment in growth is not a matter of choosing one over the other but finding a sustainable balance. Budget cuts can help control government spending and ensure that debt levels remain manageable, but without adequate investment in growth, these measures can lead to stagnation. Conversely, investment in key areas like infrastructure, education, and technology can drive long-term economic prosperity, but must be done in a manner that does not lead to unsustainable debt levels. A thoughtful approach to fiscal policy should include both prudent management of spending and strategic investments that create the conditions for future growth and competitiveness.

The Future of America's Fiscal Policies

The future of America's fiscal policies is poised to navigate a complex landscape of growing debt, changing demographics, and evolving global economic challenges. As the United States faces a rapidly expanding national debt, coupled with increased demands for public services such as healthcare and social security, the need for comprehensive fiscal reforms has never been more critical. Moving forward, the U.S. will have to make difficult choices about how to balance the need for government spending with the imperative of maintaining fiscal responsibility. The fiscal policies adopted in the coming years will have significant consequences not only for the U.S. economy but also for the nation's global economic standing.

One of the key challenges for future fiscal policy will be addressing the nation's rising national debt, which has been steadily increasing for decades. As of recent years, U.S. government debt has surpassed $30 trillion, and interest payments on this debt continue to rise. The high levels of national debt create long-term risks, such as increased borrowing costs and the potential for inflation. Future fiscal policies will need to focus on reducing the deficit and curbing the national debt growth while also ensuring that the economy remains competitive and vibrant. This may require a delicate balancing act between cutting spending, particularly in non-essential areas, and maintaining key investments in infrastructure, education, and research, which are crucial for long-term economic growth.

Another pressing issue will be entitlement reform, particularly in relation to Social Security, Medicare, and Medicaid. With the aging Baby Boomer generation, the cost of entitlement programs is set to rise significantly in the coming decades, putting immense pressure on the federal budget. The increasing demand for healthcare and social security benefits for retirees could lead to unsustainable spending if reforms are not implemented. Policymakers will need to explore ways to ensure the solvency of these programs, whether through raising the retirement age, adjusting benefit formulas, or finding new revenue streams. These decisions will be politically difficult, as they will likely require sacrifices from certain groups of the population. However, without reform, the future fiscal burden on the working-age population will be unbearable, risking economic instability.

At the same time, future fiscal policies will need to account for the changing dynamics of the global economy. The rise of emerging markets, especially China and India, and the increasing interconnectedness of global markets will influence how America approaches trade and foreign policy. Economic diplomacy, trade agreements, and tariffs will continue to shape the U.S.'s fiscal policies, particularly as new geopolitical challenges emerge. America's fiscal strategy will need to address global trade imbalances, ensure access to key international markets, and adapt to the pressures of a multipolar world order. Fiscal policies may need to promote innovation, investment in emerging industries, and ensure that the U.S. remains a leader in critical areas such as technology, manufacturing, and clean energy.

Additionally, the future of fiscal policies will be shaped by shifting priorities on both domestic and international fronts. There will likely be increased focus on climate change, income inequality, and social justice, which will require significant government investment in green technologies, affordable housing, and healthcare. However, these ambitious goals must be balanced with fiscal prudence to avoid exacerbating the national debt. Tax reform will be a key part of the discussion. Policymakers will need to decide whether to increase taxes on corporations and the wealthiest individuals to fund public programs or find alternative revenue sources. The issue of progressive taxation will likely be a hotly debated topic, as different political ideologies propose varying approaches to ensure that all citizens contribute fairly to the nation's fiscal health.

Finally, the ability of the U.S. to maintain fiscal flexibility in the face of unforeseen crises, such as pandemics, natural disasters, or international conflicts, will require forward-thinking policies that create economic resilience. While short-term government spending to stimulate the economy during crises can be necessary, the U.S. must find ways to ensure that these emergency expenditures do not permanently destabilize the fiscal system. Building a robust fiscal framework that can absorb shocks while maintaining long-term sustainability will be essential for the country's ability to thrive in an unpredictable world.

In conclusion, the future of America's fiscal policies will require a careful balance between addressing immediate economic challenges and ensuring long-term sustainability. Reducing national debt, reforming entitlement programs, promoting innovation, and navigating the changing global landscape will be key to shaping a prosperous future. With the right policies, the U.S. can ensure that it remains competitive, resilient, and capable of addressing the needs of its citizens without sacrificing fiscal responsibility. However, these challenges will require strong leadership, bipartisan cooperation, and a willingness to make tough decisions that prioritize the nation's future economic health.

Chapter 10
Looking Ahead: A New Era of Global Prosperity?

As the world emerges from a period of significant economic disruption, marked by global trade wars, the COVID-19 pandemic, and geopolitical tensions, the question of whether a new era of global prosperity is on the horizon remains a central point of discussion. The global economy is undergoing a profound transformation, driven by rapid technological advancements, shifts in international power dynamics, and evolving consumer behavior. While some regions are poised for significant growth, others face persistent challenges such as income inequality, climate change, and political instability. As nations look to recover and rebuild, the opportunities for a new era of prosperity will depend largely on how they navigate these interconnected challenges and harness the forces of innovation, cooperation, and sustainability.

Technological advancements, particularly in fields like artificial intelligence, renewable energy, and biotechnology, have the potential to drive unprecedented economic growth in the coming decades. Countries that invest in these industries and develop the necessary infrastructure to support innovation are likely to see significant improvements in productivity, efficiency, and competitiveness. The digital revolution, which has already transformed industries from healthcare to finance, will continue to reshape the global economic landscape, creating new opportunities for businesses, workers, and consumers alike. However, the benefits of these technological advancements must be shared equitably to avoid exacerbating existing inequalities between developed and developing nations. For a truly prosperous global economy, there must be concerted efforts to ensure that all countries have access to the tools and knowledge needed to thrive in a digital-first world.

At the same time, the path to global prosperity will require greater international collaboration. Global challenges such as climate change, public health crises, and the need for sustainable development cannot be solved by any one nation alone. Cooperation between governments, businesses, and civil society will be essential to address these issues and build a more resilient global economy. As trade relations evolve and new economic models emerge, countries will need to find common ground in areas such as climate policy, economic development, and fair trade practices. This chapter will explore whether the world is entering a new era of prosperity, and what actions must be taken to ensure that this prosperity is inclusive, sustainable, and beneficial for all.

The Legacy of Trumponomics

The legacy of *Trumponomics* is a complex and multifaceted one, marked by significant economic shifts, bold policy decisions, and a reevaluation of the U.S.'s role in the global economic system. At its core, *Trumponomics* was built on the principles of tax cuts, deregulation, protectionism, and a focus on prioritizing American workers. Under the Trump administration, these policies aimed to spur economic growth, reduce the trade deficit, and bring manufacturing jobs back to the United States. While some of these goals were achieved in the short term, the long-term impact of these economic policies remains a subject of debate. As the U.S. looks to the future, the lasting effects of *Trumponomics* will shape not only domestic economic policies but also the global economic landscape.

One of the most immediate and widely debated aspects of Trumponomics was the 2017 Tax Cuts and Jobs Act, which drastically reduced the corporate tax rate and provided tax cuts for individuals. Proponents of these tax cuts argued that reducing taxes would stimulate business investment, increase wages, and create jobs. Corporate tax cuts, in particular, were designed to make U.S. companies more competitive globally by incentivizing them to repatriate overseas profits and reinvest them in the U.S. economy. While there was some short-term economic growth, with a surge in stock market performance and corporate profits, critics argue that the tax cuts disproportionately benefited the wealthy and did little to address structural issues such as income inequality. The tax cuts also contributed significantly to the growing national debt, which increased during Trump's presidency, raising concerns about long-term fiscal sustainability.

Another central pillar of *Trumponomics* was the focus on deregulation, particularly in industries such as energy, finance, and manufacturing. Trump's administration rolled back numerous environmental regulations and restrictions on financial institutions, arguing that these were stifling economic growth and job creation. Deregulation in the energy sector, for example, led to an increase in domestic oil and gas production, contributing to the U.S. becoming a net exporter of energy for the first time in decades. While deregulation helped to reduce costs for businesses and promote certain industries, it also sparked criticism over the long-term environmental and social consequences. The rollback of environmental protections, especially regarding climate change, was a point of contention, with critics arguing that it compromised public health and hindered efforts to transition to a sustainable energy future.

Protectionist trade policies, perhaps the most contentious aspect of *Trumponomics*, reshaped global trade dynamics. The Trump administration's aggressive stance on trade, characterized by tariffs on Chinese goods and the renegotiation of trade agreements like NAFTA, marked a sharp departure from previous administrations' more free-market approach. The trade war with China was one of the most high-profile examples of Trump's protectionism, as the administration imposed tariffs on hundreds of billions of dollars worth of Chinese goods, arguing that China's trade practices were unfair and harmed American industries. While the tariffs led to some short-term gains in certain industries, they also resulted in retaliatory tariffs from China and other countries, disrupting global supply chains and leading to higher prices for U.S. consumers. The long-term impact of these protectionist measures remains unclear, with some economists warning that they could have adverse effects on global trade and economic cooperation.

The legacy of *Trumponomics* also includes a shift in the U.S.'s approach to global leadership. Trump's "America First" agenda, which prioritized national interests over multilateral cooperation, marked a departure from previous U.S. foreign economic policies. The withdrawal from the Trans-Pacific Partnership (TPP), the Paris Climate Agreement, and the World Health Organization (WHO) were all part of this broader strategy of disengagement from global institutions and agreements. While this approach resonated with many American voters who felt that global trade and foreign alliances were detrimental to domestic interests, it also led to tensions with traditional allies and a weakening of international partnerships. The long-term impact of this shift in U.S. foreign policy could reshape the global order, as countries like China and the European Union have increasingly sought to fill the void left by the U.S.

In the broader context, the legacy of *Trumponomics* will be remembered for its focus on stimulating short-term economic growth while raising concerns about the sustainability of those gains. While the tax cuts and deregulation policies spurred immediate economic activity, the long-term effects on income inequality, environmental sustainability, and the national debt remain contentious. The protectionist trade policies, while attempting to prioritize American industries, have left lasting disruptions in global trade and may contribute to a more fragmented and volatile economic environment in the future. Ultimately, the legacy of *Trumponomics* is one of economic populism and nationalism, with both successes and challenges that will continue to influence the direction of U.S. economic policy and global economic relations for years to come.

Potential Risks and Rewards for Global Markets

The potential risks and rewards for global markets are shaped by a multitude of factors, from geopolitical tensions and shifts in trade policies to technological advancements and global economic trends. As the global economy continues to evolve, understanding these dynamics is essential for businesses, investors, and policymakers. The risks and rewards faced by global markets are not isolated but are interconnected, with changes in one area often reverberating through others, creating both opportunities and challenges on a worldwide scale.

One of the most significant risks for global markets is the rise of economic protectionism, which has gained traction in recent years. The policies of *Trumponomics*, characterized by tariffs, trade wars, and a focus on national interests, highlighted how protectionist measures can disrupt international trade and investment. The ongoing trade tensions between the U.S. and China, for example, created significant uncertainty in global markets. Trade wars can lead to retaliatory tariffs, hurting businesses that rely on global supply chains and increasing costs for consumers. These disruptions not only affect the economies of the countries involved but can also lead to a slowdown in global trade, reducing overall economic growth. If protectionism spreads further, it could fragment global markets, leading to reduced cross-border investments and a shift toward more localized economies. This would have long-term implications for the efficiency of global markets and could dampen the economic growth prospects for emerging markets, which rely heavily on international trade.

Another risk for global markets is geopolitical instability. Political instability, conflicts, and military tensions in key regions can significantly impact investor confidence and disrupt global markets. For instance, instability in the Middle East can affect oil prices, while tensions in Europe can threaten the stability of the European Union and impact the eurozone's economic performance. Geopolitical risks can lead to volatility in financial markets, with investors becoming more risk-averse and seeking safe-haven assets like gold or U.S. Treasury bonds. Prolonged instability in major economic regions can also result in supply chain disruptions and the reallocation of global resources, as businesses and governments seek to mitigate the impact of conflict on their operations.

Despite these risks, there are substantial rewards that global markets can achieve, especially in areas driven by technological innovation and collaboration. The continued advancement of technology, particularly in artificial intelligence (AI), renewable energy, and biotechnology, has the potential to revolutionize industries and create new opportunities for economic growth. AI, for example, can drive efficiency across sectors like manufacturing, healthcare, and logistics, significantly increasing productivity and reducing operational costs. Similarly, the push toward renewable energy solutions can create new markets and industries, offering substantial opportunities for investment in clean technologies and infrastructure. Nations that invest in these sectors may reap long-term economic benefits, positioning themselves as leaders in the global economy and helping to address pressing challenges such as climate change.

Moreover, the growing trend of globalization, despite the risks of protectionism, continues to provide rewards for global markets. As emerging markets grow and expand, they represent a vast pool of consumers and labor, offering businesses new opportunities to access previously untapped markets. The rising middle class in countries like China and India, for instance, has driven demand for a wide range of goods and services, boosting global trade and creating new sources of revenue for multinational corporations. These markets offer the potential for businesses to scale operations and achieve higher profits by tapping into consumer bases that are rapidly growing and evolving. In addition, global supply chains remain an efficient way for businesses to access resources and labor at lower costs, leading to enhanced profitability and economic growth.

The expansion of global digital networks and e-commerce platforms also presents significant rewards for global markets. The digital economy has seen exponential growth in recent years, driven by increasing internet penetration, mobile technology, and cloud computing. The growth of e-commerce has allowed businesses to access a global customer base, while also enabling consumers to access a wider variety of goods at lower prices. Furthermore, digital platforms have provided entrepreneurs with the tools and resources to start businesses and expand them internationally, creating new wealth and innovation on a global scale.

In conclusion, global markets face a delicate balance of risks and rewards. Protectionism, geopolitical instability, and economic fragmentation pose significant challenges that can disrupt trade and slow economic growth. However, the continued advancement of technology, the expansion of global digital networks, and the growing opportunities in emerging markets present substantial rewards. Navigating these risks and rewards will require careful policy decisions, collaboration between nations, and strategic investments in key sectors. By harnessing the potential of innovation while addressing the risks of instability, global markets can continue to evolve and drive prosperity in an interconnected world.

Conclusion

America's role in shaping a new economic order has been central to the global economic landscape for over a century. As the world navigates a period of unprecedented challenges and opportunities—ranging from technological advancements and climate change to shifting geopolitical dynamics—the United States continues to wield considerable influence over the direction of the global economy. While the nature of that influence has evolved in recent years, America's ability to shape a new economic order remains paramount. However, the question is not just about maintaining that influence, but also how the U.S. chooses to exercise its power in a rapidly changing world.

One of the defining characteristics of America's role in shaping the global economy is its historical commitment to open markets, liberal economic policies, and multilateral institutions. After World War II, the U.S. played a key role in establishing the Bretton Woods system, which created the International Monetary Fund (IMF), the World Bank, and the General Agreement on Tariffs and Trade (GATT), later evolving into the World Trade Organization (WTO). These institutions were designed to promote international trade, stability, and growth. By championing open trade and investment, the U.S. helped create a global economic system that contributed to unprecedented growth, lifting millions of people out of poverty and driving technological and industrial innovation. America's leadership in these areas fostered a period of relatively stable global economic growth, which saw the rise of emerging economies and the expansion of the global middle class.

In recent years, however, America's role in shaping the economic order has become more complicated. The rise of new global powers, particularly China, and the shift toward more protectionist and nationalist economic policies under the Trump administration have led to a reevaluation of the U.S.'s approach to global leadership. The trade wars, withdrawal from multilateral agreements like the Paris Climate Accord and the Trans-Pacific Partnership (TPP), and a more inward-focused economic agenda marked a significant departure from previous U.S. policy. This shift has left a power vacuum in some areas of the global economy, as countries like China and the European Union step in to promote their own vision of global governance. China, with its Belt and Road Initiative (BRI) and growing influence in institutions like the Asian Infrastructure Investment Bank (AIIB), has positioned itself as a challenger to the U.S.-led liberal order.

Despite these changes, the U.S. remains an essential player in the global economic system. Its economic size, technological prowess, and military power continue to influence global markets and security. The U.S. dollar remains the world's primary reserve currency, and American financial markets are central to global trade and investment. Moreover, America is home to some of the world's largest and most innovative companies, particularly in technology, finance, and healthcare. As new industries like artificial intelligence, renewable energy, and biotechnology emerge, the U.S. has the opportunity to lead in shaping these sectors and creating new global standards.

However, America's leadership in the new economic order will depend on how it navigates the challenges of the 21st century. In an increasingly multipolar world, where power is diffusing to other regions, the U.S. must decide whether it will maintain its hegemonic role or embrace a more cooperative, multilateral approach to global governance. One of the key areas where America can shape the future of the global economy is in technology and innovation. As countries race to develop new technologies in areas like AI, quantum computing, and green energy, the U.S. must ensure it remains at the forefront of these industries. By investing in research and development, promoting digital infrastructure, and encouraging entrepreneurship, the U.S. can help create a global economic order that fosters innovation, sustainability, and equitable growth.

Moreover, addressing global challenges such as climate change, income inequality, and public health will require international collaboration. The U.S. has the potential to play a leading role in forging international agreements and promoting global standards that tackle these pressing issues. By leading the way in addressing climate change through investments in clean energy, carbon reduction technologies, and sustainable practices, America can help shape a future global economy that prioritizes environmental sustainability alongside economic growth.

Finally, America's role in the new economic order will also depend on its ability to maintain internal cohesion. As the U.S. faces increasing political polarization and economic inequality, it must address these issues at home in order to maintain its credibility on the global stage. A strong, united America—one that invests in education, infrastructure, and healthcare—will be better positioned to lead in shaping a new economic order that benefits all people, both domestically and internationally.

In conclusion, America's role in shaping a new economic order is both a challenge and an opportunity. While the global landscape has shifted in recent years, the U.S. remains a central player in driving global economic policy and shaping the future of the global economy.

By embracing innovation, fostering international cooperation, and addressing domestic challenges, the U.S. can continue to play a leading role in creating a prosperous, sustainable, and inclusive global economic system for the future.

Printed in the USA
CPSIA information can be obtained
at www.ICGtesting.com
CBHW061539111224
18825CB00039B/1304